Rand McNally

Atlas for Today's World

D1532827

Table of Contents

Published and printed in the United States.
Library of Congress Catalog Number: 95-068745

RAND McNALLY

THE UNIVERSE AND SOLAR SYSTEM

The Milky Way Galaxy

Our star, the Sun, is one of 200 billion stars banded together in the enormous gravitational spiral nebula called the Milky Way Galaxy, which is but one of millions of known galaxies in the universe.

The Milky Way is huge; it would take light — which travels at 186,000 miles per second — 100,000 years to go from one end of the galaxy to the other. In addition to the billions of stars, Earth shares the Milky Way with eight other known planets.

Statistical Data for the Milky Way Galaxy

Diameter: 100,000 light-years

Mass: About 200 billion suns

Distance between spiral arms: 6,500 light years

Thickness of galactic disk: 1,300 light-years

Satellite galaxies: 2 (visible only in the southern sky)

Sun

The Sun's diameter — more than 865,000 miles — is 109 times greater than that of the Earth. Even so, the Sun is actually a fairly small star. Somewhere in the vastness of the universe astronomers have located a star that is 3,500 times larger than the Sun.

Diameter: 865,000 miles (1,392,000 km)
Mass: 333,000 times that of the Earth
Surface temperature: 10,300° F (5,700° C)
Central temperature: 27 million° F (15 million° C)
Composition: 70% hydrogen, 27% helium
Spin (at equator): 26 days, 21 hours

Mercury

Distance from the Sun: 35,985,000 miles (57,909,000 km), or 39% that of the Earth
Diameter: 3,031 miles (4,878 km), or 38% that of the Earth
Average surface temperature: 340° F (171° C)
Atmosphere: Extremely thin, contains helium and hydrogen
Length of day: 58 days, 15 hours, 30 minutes
Length of year: 87.97 days
Satellites: None

Venus

Distance from the Sun: 67,241,000 miles (108,209,000 km), or 72% that of the Earth
Diameter: 7,521 miles (12,104 km), or 95% that of the Earth
Surface temperature: 867° F (464° C)
Surface pressure: 90 times that of the Earth, equivalent to the pressure at a water depth of 3,000 feet (900 meters)
Atmosphere: 96% carbon dioxide
Length of day: 243 days, 14 minutes. The planet spins opposite to the rotation of the Earth.
Length of year: 224.7 days
Satellites: None

Earth

Distance from the Sun: 92,960,000 miles (149,598,000 km)
Diameter: 7,926 miles (12,756 km)
Average surface temperature: 58° F (14° C)
Surface pressure: 1 atmosphere
Atmosphere: 78% nitrogen, 21% oxygen
Length of day: 23 hours, 56 minutes and 4 seconds
Length of year: 365.25 days
Satellites: 1

The Moon

The Moon is the Earth's only natural satellite. About 2,160 miles (3,746 km) across, the Moon is an airless, waterless world just one-fourth the size of the Earth. It circles the planet once every 27 days at an average distance of about 238,000 miles (384,000 km).

Mars

Distance from the Sun: 141,642,000 miles (227,940,000 km), about 1.5 times that of the Earth
Diameter: 4,222 miles (6,794 km), or 53% that of the Earth
Average surface temperature: −13° F (−25° C)
Surface pressure: 0.7% (1/150 th) that of the Earth
Atmosphere: 95% carbon dioxide, 2.7% nitrogen
Length of day: 24 hours, 37 minutes
Length of year: 1 year, 321.73 days

Jupiter

By any measure, Jupiter is the solar system's giant. To equal Jupiter's bulk would take 318 Earths. Over 1,300 Earth-sized balls could fit within this enormous planet.

Satellites: 2
Distance from the Sun: 483,631,000 miles (778,292,000 km), or 5.2 times that of the Earth
Diameter: 88,700 miles (142,800 km), or 11.3 times that of the Earth
Temperature at cloud tops: −234° F (−148° C)

Spatial Relationships of the Sun and the Planets

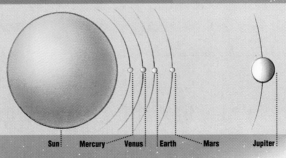

Sun   Mercury   Venus   Earth   Mars   Jupiter   Saturn

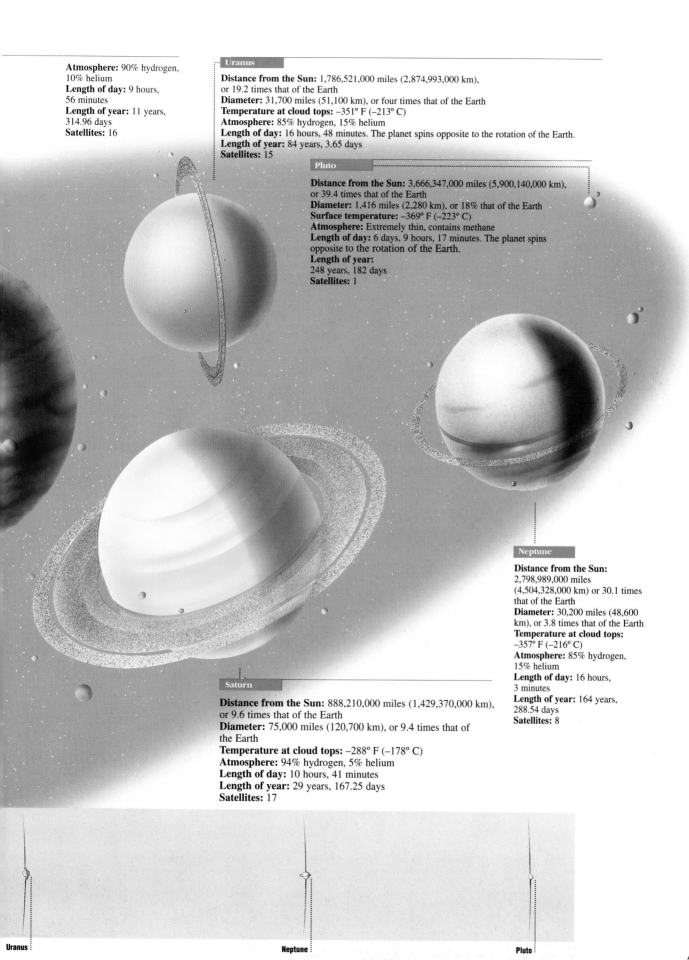

Atmosphere: 90% hydrogen, 10% helium
Length of day: 9 hours, 56 minutes
Length of year: 11 years, 314.96 days
Satellites: 16

Uranus

Distance from the Sun: 1,786,521,000 miles (2,874,993,000 km), or 19.2 times that of the Earth
Diameter: 31,700 miles (51,100 km), or four times that of the Earth
Temperature at cloud tops: −351° F (−213° C)
Atmosphere: 85% hydrogen, 15% helium
Length of day: 16 hours, 48 minutes. The planet spins opposite to the rotation of the Earth.
Length of year: 84 years, 3.65 days
Satellites: 15

Pluto

Distance from the Sun: 3,666,347,000 miles (5,900,140,000 km), or 39.4 times that of the Earth
Diameter: 1,416 miles (2,280 km), or 18% that of the Earth
Surface temperature: −369° F (−223° C)
Atmosphere: Extremely thin, contains methane
Length of day: 6 days, 9 hours, 17 minutes. The planet spins opposite to the rotation of the Earth.
Length of year: 248 years, 182 days
Satellites: 1

Neptune

Distance from the Sun: 2,798,989,000 miles (4,504,328,000 km) or 30.1 times that of the Earth
Diameter: 30,200 miles (48,600 km), or 3.8 times that of the Earth
Temperature at cloud tops: −357° F (−216° C)
Atmosphere: 85% hydrogen, 15% helium
Length of day: 16 hours, 3 minutes
Length of year: 164 years, 288.54 days
Satellites: 8

Saturn

Distance from the Sun: 888,210,000 miles (1,429,370,000 km), or 9.6 times that of the Earth
Diameter: 75,000 miles (120,700 km), or 9.4 times that of the Earth
Temperature at cloud tops: −288° F (−178° C)
Atmosphere: 94% hydrogen, 5% helium
Length of day: 10 hours, 41 minutes
Length of year: 29 years, 167.25 days
Satellites: 17

Uranus

Neptune

Pluto

THE EARTH

History of the Earth

Estimated age of the Earth:
At least 4.6 billion (4,600,000,000) years.

Formation of the Earth:
It is generally thought that the Earth was formed from a cloud of gas and dust (A) revolving around the early Sun. Gravitational forces pulled the cloud's particles together into an ever denser mass (B), with heavier particles sinking to the center. Heat from radioactive elements caused the materials of the embryonic Earth to melt and gradually settle into core and mantle layers. As the surface cooled, a crust formed. Volcanic activity released vast amounts of steam, carbon dioxide and other gases from the Earth's interior. The steam condensed into water to form the oceans, and the gases, prevented by gravity from escaping, formed the beginnings of the atmosphere (C).

The calm appearance of our planet today (D) belies the intense heat of its interior and the violent tectonic forces which are constantly reshaping its surface.

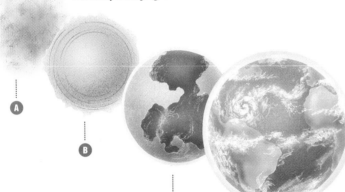

Periods in Earth's history

Earth's history is divided into different **eras**, which are subdivided into **periods**.

The most recent periods are themselves subdivided into **epochs**. The main divisions and subdivisions are shown below.

	Began	Ended	
	(million years ago)		
Precambrian Era			
Archean Period	3,800	2,500	Start of life
Proterozoic Period	2,500	590	Life in the seas
Paleozoic Era			
Cambrian Period	590	500	Sea life
Ordovician Period	505	438	First fishes
Silurian Period	438	408	First land plants
Devonian Period	408	360	Amphibians
Carboniferous Period	360	286	First reptiles
Permian Period	286	248	Spread of reptiles
Mesozoic Era			
Triassic Period	248	213	Reptiles and early mammals
Jurassic Period	213	144	Dinosaurs
Cretaceous Period	144	65	Dinosaurs, dying out at the end
Cenozoic Era			
Tertiary Period			
Paleocene	65	55	Large mammals
Eocene	55	38	Primates begin
Oligocene	38	25	Development of primates
Miocene	25	5	Modern-type animals
Pliocene	5	2	*Australopithecus* ape, ancestor to the human race
Quaternary Period			
Pleistocene	2	0.01	Ice ages; true humans
Holocene	0.01	Present	Modern humans

Source: *Atlas of the Universe* by Patrick Moore, Reed International Books Limited, 1994.

Internal Structure of the Earth

In its simplest form, the Earth is composed of a crust, a mantle with an upper and lower layer, and a core, which has an inner region.

Temperatures in the Earth increase with depth, as is observed in a deep mine shaft or borehole, but the prediction of temperatures within the Earth is made difficult by the fact that different rocks conduct heat at different rates: rock salt, for example, has 10 times the heat conductivity of coal. Also, estimates have to take into account the abundance of heat-generating atoms in a rock. Radioactive atoms are concentrated toward the Earth's surface, so the planet has, in effect, a thermal blanket to keep it warm. The temperature at the center of the Earth is believed to be approximately 5,400° F (3,000° C).

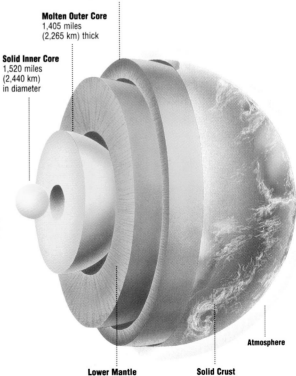

Upper Mantle
415 miles
(667 km) thick

Molten Outer Core
1,405 miles
(2,265 km) thick

Solid Inner Core
1,520 miles
(2,440 km)
in diameter

Atmosphere

Lower Mantle
1,365 miles
(2,200 km) thick

Solid Crust
0–19 miles
(0–33 km) thick

Chemical composition of the Earth:

The chemical composition of the Earth varies from crust to core. The upper crust of continents, called sial, is mainly granite, rich in aluminum and silicon. Oceanic crust, or sima, is largely basalt, made of magnesium and silicon. The mantle is composed of rocks that are rich in magnesium and iron silicates, whereas the core, it is believed, is made of iron and nickel oxides.

- Sial
- Sima
- Upper Mantle
- Lower Mantle
- Outer Core
- Inner Core

A. Silicon
B. Aluminum
C. Iron
D. Calcium
E. Magnesium
F. Nickel
G. Other

Sial (upper crust of continents)

%	A	B	C	D	E	F	G

Sima (oceanic crust)

%	A	B	C	D	E	F	G

Mantle

%	A	B	C	D	E	F	G

Core

%	A	B	C	D	E	F	G

Measurements of the Earth

Equatorial circumference of the Earth: 24,901.45 miles (40,066.43 km)

Polar circumference of the Earth: 24,855.33 miles (39,992.22 km)

Equatorial diameter of the Earth: 7,926.38 miles (12,753.54 km)

Polar diameter of the Earth: 7,899.80 miles (12,710.77 km)

Equatorial radius of the Earth: 3,963.19 miles (6,376.77 km)

Polar radius of the Earth: 3,949.90 miles (6,355.38 km)

Estimated weight of the Earth: 6,600,000,000,000,000,000,000,000 tons, or 6,600 billion billion tons (5,940 billion billion metric tons)

Total surface area of the Earth: 197,000,000 square miles (510,230,000 sq km)

Total land area of the Earth (including inland water and Antarctica): 57,900,000 square miles (150,100,000 sq km)

Total ocean area of the Earth: 139,200,000 square miles (360,528,000 sq km), or 70% of the Earth's surface area

Total area of the Earth's surface covered with water (oceans and all inland water): 147,750,000 square miles (382,672,500 sq km), or 75% of the Earth's surface area

Types of water: 97% of the Earth's water is salt water; 3% is fresh water

Life on Earth

Number of plant species on Earth: About 350,000

Number of animal species on Earth: More than one million

Estimated total human population of the Earth: 5,628,000,000

Movements of the Earth

Mean distance of the Earth from the Sun: About 93 million miles (149.6 million km)

Period in which the Earth makes one complete orbit around the Sun: 365 days, 5 hours, 48 minutes, and 46 seconds

Speed of the Earth as it orbits the Sun: 66,700 miles (107,320 km) per hour

Period in which the Earth makes one complete rotation on its axis: 23 hours, 56 minutes and 4 seconds

Equatorial speed at which the Earth rotates on its axis: More than 1,000 miles (1,600 km) per hour

The Shape of the Earth
Comparing the Earth's equatorial and polar dimensions reveals that our planet is actually not a perfect sphere but rather an oblate spheroid, flattened at the poles and bulging at the equator. This is the result of a combination of gravitational and centrifugal forces.

An even more precise term for the Earth's shape is "geoid" — the actual shape of sea level, which is lumpy, with variations away from spheroid of up to 260 feet (80 m). This lumpiness reflects major variations in density in the Earth's outer layers.

The Seasons
(Northern Hemisphere)

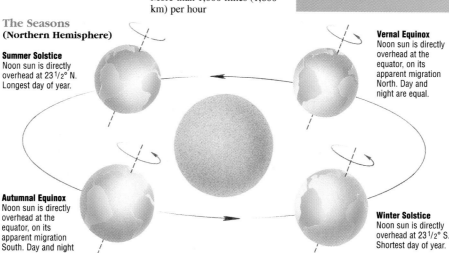

Summer Solstice
Noon sun is directly overhead at 23 1/2° N. Longest day of year.

Vernal Equinox
Noon sun is directly overhead at the equator, on its apparent migration North. Day and night are equal.

Autumnal Equinox
Noon sun is directly overhead at the equator, on its apparent migration South. Day and night are equal.

Winter Solstice
Noon sun is directly overhead at 23 1/2° S. Shortest day of year.

CONTINENTS AND ISLANDS

The word "continents" designates the largest continuous masses of land in the world.

For reasons that are mainly historical, seven continents are generally recognized: Africa, Antarctica, Asia, Australia, Europe, North America, and South America. Since Asia and Europe actually share the same land mass, they are sometimes identified as a single continent, Eurasia.

The lands of the central and south Pacific, including Australia, New Zealand, Micronesia, Melanesia, and Polynesia, are sometimes grouped together as Oceania.

The Continents

Africa

Area in square miles (sq km):
11,700,000 (30,300,000)
Estimated population (Jan. 1, 1995):
697,600,000
Population per square mile (sq km):
60 (23)
Mean elevation in feet (meters):
1,900 (580)
Highest elevation in feet (meters):
Kilimanjaro, Tanzania, 19,340 (5,895)
Lowest elevation in feet (meters):
Lac Assal, Djibouti, 515 (157) below sea level

Antarctica

Area in square miles (sq km):
5,400,000 (14,000,000)
Estimated population (Jan. 1, 1995):
Uninhabited
Population per square mile (sq km):
0 (0)
Mean elevation in feet (meters):
6,000 (1,830)
Highest elevation in feet (meters):
Vinson Massif, 16,066 (4,897)
Lowest elevation in feet (meters):
sea level

Asia

Area in square miles (sq km):
17,300,000 (44,900,000)
Estimated population (Jan. 1, 1995):
3,422,700,000
Population per square mile (sq km):
198 (76)
Mean elevation in feet (meters):
3,000 (910)
Highest elevation in feet (meters):
Mt. Everest, China (Nepal)–Tibet, 29,028 (8,848)
Lowest elevation in feet (meters):
Dead Sea, Israel–Jordan,
1,339 (408) below sea level

Australia

Area in square miles (sq km):
2,966,155 (7,682,300)
Estimated population (Jan. 1, 1995):
18,205,000
Population per square mile (sq km):
6.1 (2.4)
Mean elevation in feet (meters):
1,000 (305)
Highest elevation in feet (meters):
Mt. Kosciusko, New South Wales, 7,310 (2,228)
Lowest elevation in feet (meters):
Lake Eyre, South Australia, 52 (16) below sea level

Europe

Area in square miles (sq km):
3,800,000 (9,900,000)
Estimated population (Jan. 1, 1995):
712,100,000
Population per square mile (sq km):
187 (72)
Mean elevation in feet (meters):
980 (300)
Highest elevation in feet (meters):
Gora El'brus, Russia, 18,510 (5,642)
Lowest elevation in feet (meters):
Caspian Sea, Asia-Europe, 92 (28) below sea level

North America

Area in square miles (sq km):
9,500,000 (24,700,000)
Estimated population (Jan. 1, 1995):
453,300,000
Population per square mile (sq km):
48 (18)
Mean elevation in feet (meters):
2,000 (610)
Highest elevation in feet (meters):
Mt. McKinley, Alaska, U.S., 20,320 (6,194)
Lowest elevation in feet (meters):
Death Valley, California, U.S.,
282 (84) below sea level

Oceania *(incl. Australia)*

Area in square miles (sq km):
3,300,000 (8,500,000)
Estimated population (Jan. 1, 1995):
28,400,000
Population per square mile (sq km):
8.6 (3.3)
Mean elevation in feet (meters):
0 (0)
Highest elevation in feet (meters):
Mt. Wilhelm, Papua New Guinea, 14,793 (4,509)
Lowest elevation in feet (meters):
Lake Eyre, South Australia, 52 (16) below sea level

South America

Area in square miles (sq km):
6,900,000 (17,800,000)
Estimated population (Jan. 1, 1995):
313,900,000
Population per square mile (sq km):
45 (18)
Mean elevation in feet (meters):
1,800 (550)
Highest elevation in feet (meters):
Cerro Aconcagua, Argentina, 22,831 (6,959)
Lowest elevation in feet (meters):
Salinas Chicas, Argentina, 138 (42) below sea level

World

Area in square miles (sq km):
57,900,000 (150,100,000)
Estimated population (Jan. 1, 1995):
5,628,000,000
Population per square mile (sq km):
97 (37)
Mean elevation in feet (meters):
0 (0)
Highest elevation in feet (meters):
Mt. Everest, China–Nepal, 29,028 (8,848)
Lowest elevation in feet (meters):
Dead Sea, Israel–Jordan,
1,339 (408) below sea level

Rank	Name	Area square miles	square km
1	Greenland, North America	840,000	2,175,600
2	New Guinea, Asia-Oceania	309,000	800,000
3	Borneo (Kalimantan), Asia	287,300	744,100
4	Madagascar, Africa	226,500	587,000
5	Baffin Island, Canada	195,928	507,451
6	Sumatra (Sumatera), Indonesia	182,860	473,606
7	Honshū, Japan	89,176	230,966
8	Great Britain, United Kingdom	88,795	229,978
9	Victoria Island, Canada	83,897	217,291
10	Ellesmere Island, Canada	75,767	196,236
11	Celebes (Sulawesi), Indonesia	73,057	189,216
12	South Island, New Zealand	57,708	149,463
13	Java (Jawa), Indonesia	51,038	132,187
14	North Island, New Zealand	44,332	114,821
15	Cuba, North America	42,800	110,800
16	Newfoundland, Canada	42,031	108,860
17	Luzon, Philippines	40,420	104,688
18	Iceland, Europe	39,800	103,000
19	Mindanao, Philippines	36,537	94,630
20	Ireland, Europe	32,600	84,400
21	Hokkaidō, Japan	32,245	83,515
22	Novaya Zemlya, Russia	31,900	82,600
23	Sakhalin, Russia	29,500	76,400
24	Hispaniola, North America	29,400	76,200
25	Banks Island, Canada	27,038	70,028
26	Tasmania, Australia	26,200	67,800
27	Sri Lanka, Asia	24,900	64,600
28	Devon Island, Canada	21,331	55,247
29	Tierra del Fuego, South America	18,600	48,200
30	Kyūshū, Japan	17,129	44,363
31	Melville Island, Canada	16,274	42,149
32	Southampton Island, Canada	15,913	41,214
33	Spitsbergen, Norway	15,260	39,523
34	New Britain, Papua New Guinea	14,093	36,500
35	Taiwan, Asia	13,900	36,000
36	Hainan Dao, China	13,100	34,000
37	Prince of Wales Island, Canada	12,872	33,339
38	Vancouver Island, Canada	12,079	31,285
39	Sicily, Italy	9,926	25,709
40	Somerset Island, Canada	9,570	24,786
41	Sardinia, Italy	9,301	24,090
42	Shikoku, Japan	7,258	18,799
43	Ceram (Seram), Indonesia	7,191	18,625
44	North East Land, Norway	6,350	16,446
45	New Caledonia, Oceania	6,252	16,192
46	Timor, Indonesia	5,743	14,874
47	Flores, Indonesia	5,502	14,250
48	Samar, Philippines	5,100	13,080
49	Negros, Philippines	4,907	12,710
50	Palawan, Philippines	4,550	11,785
51	Panay, Philippines	4,446	11,515
52	Jamaica, North America	4,200	11,000
53	Hawaii, United States	4,034	10,448
54	Cape Breton Island, Canada	3,981	10,311
55	Mindoro, Philippines	3,759	9,735
56	Kodiak Island, United States	3,670	9,505
57	Bougainville, Papua New Guinea	3,600	9,300
58	Cyprus, Asia	3,572	9,251
59	Puerto Rico, North America	3,500	9,100
60	New Ireland, Papua New Guinea	3,500	9,000
61	Corsica (Corse), France	3,367	8,720
62	Crete, Greece	3,189	8,259
63	Vrangelya, Ostrov (Wrangel Island), Russia	2,800	7,300
64	Leyte, Philippines	2,785	7,214
65	Guadalcanal, Solomon Islands	2,060	5,336
66	Long Island, New York, United States	1,377	3,566

Islands, Islands, Everywhere

Four islands — Hokkaidō, Honshū, Kyūshū, and Shikoku —
constitute 98% of Japan's total land area, but the country is actually
comprised of more than 3,000 islands. Similarly, two islands —
Great Britain and Ireland — make up 93% of the total land area of
the British Isles, but the island group also includes more than 5,000
smaller islands.

Greenland
New Guinea
Borneo
Madagascar
Baffin Island
Sumatra
Honshū
Great Britain
Victoria Island
Ellesmere Island

Major World Island Groups

Aleutian Islands (Pacific Ocean)

Alexander Archipelago
(Pacific Ocean)

Azores (Atlantic Ocean)

Bahamas (Atlantic Ocean)

Balearic Islands
(Mediterranean Sea)

British Isles (Atlantic Ocean)

Bismarck Archipelago
(Pacific Ocean)

Canary Islands (Atlantic Ocean)

Cape Verde Islands
(Atlantic Ocean)

Dodecanese (Mediterranean Sea)

Faeroe Islands (Atlantic Ocean)

Falkland Islands (Atlantic Ocean)

Fiji Islands (Pacific Ocean)

Galapagos Islands (Pacific Ocean)

Greater Sunda Islands (Indian/Pacific
Oceans)

Hawaiian Islands (Pacific Ocean)

Ionian Islands
(Mediterranean Sea)

Japan (Pacific Ocean)

Kikládhes (Mediterranean Sea)

Kuril Islands (Pacific Ocean)

Lesser Sunda Islands
(Indian Ocean)

Moluccas (Pacific Ocean)

New Hebrides (Atlantic Ocean)

New Siberian Islands
(Arctic Ocean)

Novaya Zemlya (Arctic Ocean)

Philippine Islands (Pacific Ocean)

Ryukyu Islands (Pacific Ocean)

Severnaya Zemlya (Arctic Ocean)

Solomon Islands (Pacific Ocean)

Spitsbergen (Arctic Ocean)

Contrasting Population Densities

Some islands are among
the most densely populated
places on Earth, while
others are among the least
densely populated. This
fact is dramatically
illustrated by
the following
comparison of
five islands:

Manhattan,
N.Y., U.S.,
(pop. 1,488,000) — 67,636/ sq mile (26,105/ sq km)

Singapore Island, Singapore
(pop. 2,921,000) — 11,874/ sq mile (4,593/ sq km)

Long Island, N.Y., U.S.
(pop. 6,863,000) — 4,984/ sq mile (1,925/ sq km)

Population per square mile (sq km)

Baffin
Island,
Canada
(pop.
8,800)
0.04/
sq mile
(0.02/
sq km)

Greenland
(pop. 57,000)
0.07/
sq mile
(0.03/
sq km)

MOUNTAINS, VOLCANOES, AND EARTHQUAKES

The Tallest Mountain in the World

With its peak reaching 29,028 feet (8,848 m) above sea level, Mt. Everest ranks as the *highest* mountain in the world, but not the *tallest*. That title goes to Mauna Kea, one of the five volcanic mountains that make up the island of Hawaii. From its base on the floor of the Pacific Ocean, Mauna Kea rises 33,476 feet (10,210 m)—more than six miles—although only the top 13,796 feet (4,205 m) are above sea level.

Seafloor Atop Mt. Everest

When Sir Edmund Percival Hillary and Tenzing Norgay reached the summit of Mt. Everest in 1953, they probably did not realize they were standing on the seafloor.

The Himalayan mountain system was formed through the process of plate tectonics. Ocean once separated India and Asia, but 180 million years ago the Indo-Australian crustal plate, on which India sits, began a northward migration and eventually collided with the Eurasian plate. The seafloor between the two land-masses crumpled and was slowly thrust upward. Rock layers that once lay at the bottom of the ocean now crown the peaks of the highest mountains in the world.

Principal Mountain Systems and Ranges of the World

Alaska Range (North America)
Alps (Europe)
Altai (Asia)
Andes (South America)
Apennines (Europe)
Atlas Mountains (Africa)
Appalachian Mountains (North America)
Brooks Range (North America)
Carpathian Mountains (Europe)
Cascade Range (North America)
Caucasus Mountains (Europe/Asia)
Coast Mountains (North America)
Coast Ranges (North America)
Great Dividing Range (Australia)
Greater Khingan Range (Asia)
Himalayas (Asia)
Hindu Kush (Asia)
Karakoram Range (Asia)
Kunlun Shan (Asia)
Madre Occidental, Sierra (North America)
Madre Oriental, Sierra (North America)
Nevada, Sierra (North America)
Pamir (Asia)
Pyrenees (Europe)
Rocky Mountains (North America)
Sayan Mountains (Asia)
Southern Alps (New Zealand)
Tien Shan (Asia)
Ural Mountains (Europe)
Zagros Mountains (Asia)

Principal Mountains of the World Δ = Highest mountain in range, region, country, or state named

Location	Height Feet	Height Meters	Location	Height Feet	Height Meters
Africa			Dufourspitze, Italy-Δ Switzerland	15,203	4,634
Kilimanjaro, Δ Tanzania (Δ Africa)	19,340	5,895	Weisshorn, Switzerland	14,783	4,506
Kirinyaga (Mount Kenya), Δ Kenya	17,058	5,199	Matterhorn, Italy-Switzerland	14,692	4,478
Margherita Peak, Δ Uganda-Δ Zaire	16,763	5,109	Finsteraarhorn, Switzerland	14,022	4,274
Ras Dashen Terara, Δ Ethiopia	15,158	4,620	Jungfrau, Switzerland	13,642	4,158
Meru, Mount, Tanzania	14,978	4,565	Écrins, Barre des, France	13,458	4,102
Karisimbi, Volcan, Δ Rwanda-Zaire	14,787	4,507	Viso, Monte, Italy (Δ Cottian Alps)	12,602	3,841
Elgon, Mount, Kenya-Uganda	14,178	4,321	Grossglockner, Δ Austria	12,457	3,797
Toubkal, Jebel, Δ Morocco (Δ Atlas Mts.)	13,665	4,165	Teide, Pico de, Δ Spain (Δ Canary Is.)	12,188	3,715
Cameroon Mountain, Δ Cameroon	13,451	4,100	**North America**		
Antarctica			McKinley, Mt., Δ Alaska		
Vinson Massif, Δ Antarctica	16,066	4,897	(Δ United States; Δ North America)	20,320	6,194
Kirkpatrick, Mount	14,856	4,528	Logan, Mt., Δ Canada		
Markham, Mount	14,272	4,350	(Δ Yukon; Δ St. Elias Mts.)	19,551	5,959
Jackson, Mount	13,747	4,190	Orizaba, Pico de, Δ Mexico	18,406	5,610
Sidley, Mount	13,717	4,181	St. Elias, Mt., Alaska-Canada	18,008	5,489
Wade, Mount	13,396	4,083	Popocatépetl, Volcán, Mexico	17,930	5,465
Asia			Foraker, Mt., Alaska	17,400	5,304
Everest, Mount, Δ China-Δ Nepal			Iztaccíhuatl, Mexico	17,159	5,230
(Δ Tibet; Δ Himalayas; Δ Asia; Δ World)	29,028	8,848	Lucania, Mt., Canada	17,147	5,226
K2 (Qogir Feng), China-Δ Pakistan			Fairweather, Mt., Alaska-Canada		
(Δ Kashmir; Δ Karakoram Range)	28,250	8,611	(Δ British Columbia)	15,300	4,663
Kanchenjunga, Δ India-Nepal	28,208	8,598	Whitney, Mt., Δ California	14,494	4,418
Makalu, China-Nepal	27,825	8,481	Elbert, Mt., Δ Colorado (Δ Rocky Mts.)	14,433	4,399
Dhawlāgiri, Nepal	26,810	8,172	Massive, Mt., Colorado	14,421	4,396
Nanga Parbat, Pakistan	26,660	8,126	Harvard, Mt., Colorado	14,420	4,395
Annapurna, Nepal	26,504	8,078	Rainier, Mt., Δ Washington		
Gasherbrum, China-Pakistan	26,470	8,068	(Δ Cascade Range)	14,410	4,392
Xixabangma Feng, China	26,286	8,012	Williamson, Mt., California	14,370	4,380
Nanda Devi, India	25,645	7,817	La Plata Pk., Colorado	14,361	4,377
Kamet, China-India	25,447	7,756	Blanca Pk., Colorado		
Namjagbarwa Feng, China	25,446	7,756	(Δ Sangre de Cristo Mts.)	14,345	4,372
Muztag, China (Δ Kunlun Shan)	25,338	7,723	Uncompahgre Pk., Colorado		
Tirich Mir, Pakistan (Δ Hindu Kush)	25,230	7,690	(Δ San Juan Mts.)	14,309	4,361
Gongga Shan, China	24,790	7,556	Grays Pk., Colorado (Δ Front Range)	14,270	4,349
Kula Kangri, Δ Bhutan	24,784	7,554	Evans, Mt., Colorado	14,264	4,348
Kommunizma, Pik, Δ Tajikistan (Δ Pamir)	24,590	7,495	Longs Pk., Colorado	14,255	4,345
Nowshak, Δ Afghanistan-Pakistan	24,557	7,485	Wrangell, Mt., Alaska	14,163	4,317
Pobedy, Pik, China-Russia	24,406	7,439	Shasta, Mt., California	14,162	4,317
Chomo Lhari, Bhutan-China	23,997	7,314	Pikes Pk., Colorado	14,110	4,301
Muztag, China	23,891	7,282	Colima, Nevado de, Mexico	13,991	4,240
Lenina, Pik, Δ Kyrgyzstan-Tajikistan	23,406	7,134	Tajumulco, Volcán, Δ Guatemala		
Api, Nepal	23,399	7,132	(Δ Central America)	13,845	4,220
Kangrinboqê Feng, China	22,028	6,714	Gannett Pk., Δ Wyoming	13,804	4,207
Hkakabo Razi, Δ Myanmar	19,296	5,881	Mauna Kea, Δ Hawaii	13,796	4,205
Damavend, Qolleh-ye, Δ Iran	18,386	5,604	Grand Teton, Wyoming	13,770	4,197
Agri Dagi			Mauna Loa, Hawaii	13,679	4,169
(Mount Ararat), Δ Turkey	16,854	5,137	Kings Pk., Δ Utah	13,528	4,123
Fuladi, Kuh-e, Afghanistan	16,847	5,135	Cloud Pk., Wyoming (Δ Bighorn Mts.)	13,167	4,013
Jaya, Puncak, Δ Indonesia (Δ New Guinea)	16,503	5,030	Waddington, Mt., Canada (Δ Coast Mts.)	13,163	4,012
Klyuchevskaya Sopka, Vulkan, Russia			Wheeler Pk., Δ New Mexico	13,161	4,011
(Δ Poluostrov Kamchatka)	15,584	4,750	Boundary Pk., Δ Nevada	13,143	4,006
Trikora, Puncak, Indonesia	15,584	4,750	Robson, Mt., Canada (Δ Canadian Rockies)	12,972	3,954
Belucha, Gora, Kazakhstan-Russia	14,783	4,506	Granite Pk., Δ Montana	12,799	3,901
Turgen, Mount, Mongolia	14,311	4,362	Borah Pk., Δ Idaho	12,662	3,859
Kinabalu, Gunong, Δ Malaysia (Δ Borneo)	13,455	4,101	Humphreys Pk., Δ Arizona	12,633	3,851
Yü Shan, Δ Taiwan	13,114	3,997	Chirripó, Volcán, Δ Costa Rica	12,530	3,819
Erciyes Dagı, Turkey	12,851	3,917	Columbia, Mt., Canada (Δ Alberta)	12,294	3,747
Kerinci, Gunung, Indonesia (Δ Sumatra)	12,467	3,800	Adams, Mt., Washington	12,276	3,742
Fuji, Mt., Δ Japan (Δ Honshu)	12,388	3,776	Gunnbjørn Fjeld, Δ Greenland	12,139	3,700
Rinjani, Gunung, Indonesia (Δ Lombok)	12,224	3,726	**South America**		
Semeru, Gunung, Indonesia (Δ Java)	12,060	3,676	Aconcagua, Cerro, Δ Argentina		
Nabi Shu'ayb, Jabal an-, Δ Yemen			(Δ Andes; Δ South America)	22,831	6,959
(Δ Arabian Peninsula)	12,008	3,660	Ojos del Salado, Nevado, Argentina-Δ Chile	22,615	6,893
Australia / Oceania			Bonete, Cerro, Argentina	22,546	6,872
Wilhelm, Mt., Δ Papua New Guinea	14,793	4,509	Huascarán, Nevado, Δ Peru	22,133	6,746
Giluwe, Mt., Papua New Guinea	14,330	4,368	Llullaillaco, Volcán, Argentina-Chile	22,110	6,739
Bangeta, Mt., Papua New Guinea	13,520	4,121	Yerupaja, Nevado, Peru	21,765	6,634
Victoria, Mt., Papua New Guinea			Tupungato, Cerro, Argentina-Chile	21,555	6,570
(Δ Owen Stanley Range)	13,238	4,035	Sajama, Nevado, Bolivia	21,463	6,542
Cook, Mt., Δ New Zealand			Illampu, Nevado, Bolivia	21,066	6,421
(Δ South Island)	12,316	3,754	Illimani, Nevado, Bolivia	20,741	6,322
Europe			Chimborazo, Δ Ecuador	20,702	6,310
El'brus, Gora, Δ Russia			Antofalla, Volcán, Argentina	20,013	6,100
(Δ Caucasus; Δ Europe)	18,510	5,642	Cotopaxi, Ecuador	19,347	5,897
Dykhtau, Mt., Russia	17,073	5,204	Misti, Volcán, Peru	19,101	5,822
Blanc, Mont (Monte Bianco) Δ France-			Huila, Nevado del, Colombia		
Δ Italy (Δ Alps)	15,771	4,807	(Δ Cordillera Central)	18,865	5,750
			Bolívar, Pico, Δ Venezuela	16,427	5,007

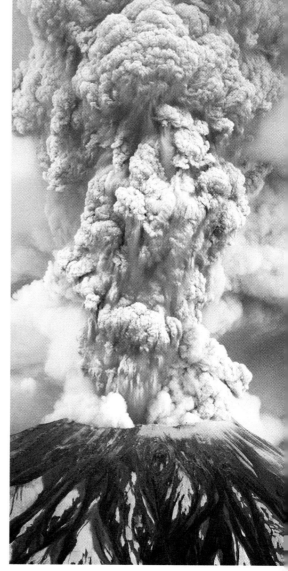

Eruption of Mt. St. Helens in 1980

Notable Volcanic Eruptions

Year	Volcano Name, Location	Comments
ca. 4895 B.C.	Crater Lake, Oregon, U.S.	Collapse forms caldera that now contains Crater Lake.
ca. 4350 B.C.	Kikai, Ryukyu Islands, Japan	Japan's largest known eruption.
ca. 1628 B.C.	Santorini (Thira), Greece	Eruption devastates late Minoan civilization.
79 A.D.	Vesuvius, Italy	Roman towns of Pompeii and Herculaneum are buried.
ca. 180	Taupo, New Zealand	Area measuring 6,200 square miles (16,000 sq km) is devastated.
ca. 260	Ilopango, El Salvador	Thousands killed, with major impact on Mayan civilization.
915	Towada, Honshu, Japan	Japan's largest historic eruption.
ca. 1000	Baitoushan, China/Korea	Largest known eruption on Asian mainland.
1259	Unknown	Evidence from polar ice cores suggests that a huge eruption, possibly the largest of the millennium, occurred in this year.
1586	Kelut, Java	Explosions in crater lake; mudflows kill 10,000.
1631	Vesuvius, Italy	Eruption kills 4,000.
ca. 1660	Long Island, Papua New Guinea	"The time of darkness" in tribal legends on Papua New Guinea.
1672	Merapi, Java	Pyroclastic flows and mudflows kill 3,000.
1711	Awu, Sangihe Islands, Indonesia	Pyroclastic flows kill 3,000.
1760	Makian, Halmahera, Indonesia	Eruption kills 2,000; island evacuated for seven years.
1772	Papandayan, Java	Debris avalanche causes 2,957 fatalities.
1783	Lakagigar, Iceland	Largest historic lava flows; 9,350 deaths.
1790	Kilauea, Hawaii	Hawaii's last large explosive eruption.
1792	Unzen, Kyushu, Japan	Tsunami and debris avalanche kill 14,500.
1815	Tambora, Indonesia	History's most explosive eruption; 92,000 deaths.
1822	Galunggung, Java	Pyroclastic flows and mudflows kill 4,011.
1856	Awu, Sangihe Islands, Indonesia	Pyroclastic flows kill 2,806.
1883	Krakatau, Indonesia	Caldera collapse; 36,417 people killed, most by tsunami.
1888	Ritter Island, Papua New Guinea	3,000 killed, most by tsunami created by debris avalanche.
1902	Mont Pelee, West Indies	Town of St. Pierre destroyed; 28,000 people killed.
1902	Santa Maria, Guatemala	5,000 killed as 10 villages are buried by volcanic debris.
1912	Novarupta (Katmai), Alaska	Largest 20th-century eruption.
1914	Lassen, California, U.S.	California's last historic eruption.
1919	Kelut, Java	Mudflows devastate 104 villages and kill 5,110 people.
1930	Merapi, Java	1,369 people are killed as 42 villages are totally or partially destroyed.
1943	Parícutin, Mexico	Fissure in cornfield erupts, building cinder cone 1,500 feet (460 m) high within two years. One of the few volcano births ever witnessed.
1951	Lamington, Papua New Guinea	Pyroclastic flows kill 2,942.
1963	Surtsey, Iceland	Submarine eruption builds new island.
1977	Nyiragongo, Zaire	One of the shortest major eruptions and fastest lava flows ever recorded.
1980	St. Helens, Washington, U.S.	Lateral blast; 230-square-mile (600 sq km) area devastated.
1982	El Chichón, Mexico	Pyroclastic surges kill 1,877.
1985	Ruiz, Colombia	Mudflows kill 23,080.
1991	Pinatubo, Luzon, Philippines	Major eruption in densely populated area prompts evacuation of 250,000 people; fatalities number fewer than 800. Enormous amount of gas released into stratosphere lowers global temperatures for more than a year.
1993	Juan de Fuca Ridge, off the coast of Oregon, U.S.	Deep submarine rift eruptions account for three-fourths of all lava produced; this is one of the very few such eruptions that have been well-documented.

Sources: Smithsonian Institution Global Volcanism Program; Volcanoes of the World, *Second Edition, by Tom Simkin and Lee Siebert, Geoscience Press and Smithsonian Institution, 1994.*

Significant Earthquakes through History

Year	Estimated Magnitude	Number of Deaths	Place
365		50,000	Knossos, Crete
844		50,000	Damascus, Syria; Antioch, Turkey
856		150,000	Dāmghān, Kashan, Qumis, Iran
893		150,000	Caucasus region
894		180,000	western India
1042		50,000	Palmyra, Baalbek, Syria
1138		230,000	Aleppo, Gansana, Syria
1139	6.8	300,000	Gandzha, Kiapas, Azerbaijan
1201		50,000	upper Egypt to Syria
1290	6.7	100,000	eastern China
1556		820,000	Shaanxi Province, China
1662		300,000	China
1667	6.9	80,000	Caucasus region, northern Iran
1668		50,000	Shandong Province, China
1693		93,000	Sicily, Italy
1727		77,000	Tabrīz, Iran
1731		100,000	Beijing, China
1739		50,000	China
1755		62,000	Morocco, Portugal, Spain
1780	6.7	100,000	Tabrīz, Iran
1868	7.7	70,000	Ecuador, Colombia
1908	7.5	83,000	Calabria, Messina, Italy
1920	8.5	200,000	Gansu and Shaanxi provinces, China
1923	8.2	142,807	Tokyo, Yokohama, Japan
1927	8.3	200,000	Gansu and Qinghai provinces, China
1932	7.6	70,000	Gansu Province, China
1970	7.8	66,794	northern Peru
1976	7.8	242,000	Tangshan, China
1990	7.7	50,000	northwestern Iran

Some Significant U.S. Earthquakes

Year	Estimated Magnitude	Number of Deaths	Place
1811–12	8.6, 8.4, 8.7	<10	New Madrid, Missouri (series)
1886	7.0	60	Charleston, South Carolina
1906	8.3	3,000	San Francisco, California
1933	6.3	115	Long Beach, California
1946	7.4	5‡	Alaska
1964	8.4	125	Anchorage, Alaska
1971	6.8	65	San Fernando, California
1989	7.1	62	San Francisco Bay Area, California
1994	6.8	58	Northridge, California

‡ A tsunami generated by this earthquake struck Hilo, Hawaii, killing 159 people.
Sources: Lowell S. Whiteside, National Geophysical Data Center; Catalog of Significant Earthquakes 2150 B.C.—1991 A.D. by Paula K. Dunbar, Patricia A. Lockridge, and Lowell S. Whiteside, National Geophysical Data Center, National Oceanic and Atmospheric Administration.

OCEANS AND LAKES

Oceans, Seas, Gulfs, and Bays

	Area sq. miles	sq. km.	Volume of water cubic miles	cubic km.	Mean depth feet	meters	Greatest known depth feet	meters	
Pacific Ocean	63,800,000	165,200,000	169,650,000	707,100,000	12,987	3,957	35,810	10,922	Mariana Trench
Atlantic Ocean	31,800,000	82,400,000	79,199,000	330,100,000	11,821	3,602	28,232	8,610	Puerto Rico Trench
Indian Ocean	28,900,000	74,900,000	68,282,000	284,600,000	12,261	3,736	23,812	7,258	Weber Basin
Arctic Ocean	5,400,000	14,000,000	4,007,000	16,700,000	3,712	1,131	17,897	5,453	Lat. 77° 45'N, long. 175°W
Coral Sea	1,850,000	4,791,000	2,752,000	11,470,000	7,857	2,394	30,079	9,165	
Arabian Sea	1,492,000	3,864,000	2,416,000	10,070,000	8,973	2,734	19,029	5,803	
South China Sea	1,331,000	3,447,000	943,000	3,929,000	3,741	1,140	18,241	5,563	
Caribbean Sea	1,063,000	2,753,000	1,646,000	6,860,000	8,175	2,491	25,197	7,685	Off Cayman Islands
Mediterranean Sea	967,000	2,505,000	901,000	3,754,000	4,916	1,498	16,470	5,023	Off Cape Matapan, Greece
Bering Sea	876,000	2,269,000	911,000	3,796,000	5,382	1,640	25,194	7,684	Off Buldir Island
Bengal, Bay of	839,000	2,173,000	1,357,000	5,616,000	8,484	2,585	17,251	5,261	
Okhotsk, Sea of	619,000	1,603,000	316,000	1,317,000	2,694	821	1,029	3,374	Lat. 146° 10'E, long. 46° 50'N
Norwegian Sea	597,000	1,546,000	578,000	2,408,000	5,717	1,742	13,189	4,022	
Mexico, Gulf of	596,000	1,544,000	560,000	2,332,000	8,205	2,500	14,370	4,382	Sigsbee Deep
Hudson Bay	475,000	1,230,000	22,000	92,000	328	100	850	259	Near entrance
Greenland Sea	465,000	1,204,000	417,000	1,740,000	4,739	1,444	15,899	4,849	
Japan, Sea of	413,000	1,070,000	391,000	1,630,000	5,037	1,535	12,041	3,669	
Arafura Sea	400,000	1,037,000	49,000	204,000	646	197	12,077	3,680	
East Siberian Sea	357,000	926,000	14,000	61,000	216	66	508	155	
Kara Sea	349,000	903,000	24,000	101,000	371	113	2,034	620	
East China Sea	290,000	752,000	63,000	263,000	1,145	349	7,778	2,370	
Banda Sea	268,000	695,000	511,000	2,129,000	10,056	3,064	24,418	7,440	
Baffin Bay	263,000	681,000	142,000	593,000	2,825	861	7,010	2,136	
Laptev Sea	262,000	678,000	87,000	363,000	1,772	540	9,780	2,980	
Timor Sea	237,000	615,000	60,000	250,000	1,332	406	10,863	3,310	
Andaman Sea	232,000	602,000	158,000	660,000	3,597	1,096	13,777	4,198	
Chukchi Sea	228,000	590,000	11,000	45,000	252	77	525	160	
North Sea	214,000	554,000	12,000	52,000	315	96	2,655	809	
Java Sea	185,000	480,000	5,000	22,000	147	45	292	89	
Beaufort Sea	184,000	476,000	115,000	478,000	3,295	1,004	12,245	3,731	
Red Sea	174,000	450,000	60,000	251,000	1,831	558	8,648	2,635	
Baltic Sea	173,000	448,000	5,000	20,000	157	48	1,506	459	
Celebes Sea	168,000	435,000	380,000	1,586,000	11,962	3,645	19,173	5,842	
Black Sea	166,000	431,000	133,000	555,000	3,839	1,170	7,256	2,211	
Yellow Sea	161,000	417,000	4,000	17,000	131	40	344	105	
Sulu Sea	134,000	348,000	133,000	553,000	5,221	1,591	18,300	5,576	
Molucca Sea	112,000	291,000	133,000	554,000	6,242	1,902	16,311	4,970	
Ceram Sea	72,000	187,000	54,000	227,000	3,968	1,209	17,456	5,319	
Flores Sea	47,000	121,000	53,000	222,000	6,003	1,829	16,813	5,123	
Bali Sea	46,000	119,000	12,000	49,000	1,349	411	4,253	1,296	
Savu Sea	41,000	105,000	43,000	178,000	5,582	1,701	11,060	3,370	
White Sea	35,000	91,000	1,000	4,400	161	49	1,083	330	
Azov, Sea of	15,000	40,000	100	400	29	9	46	14	
Marmara, Sea of	4,000	11,000	1,000	4,000	1,171	357	4,138	1,261	

Source: Atlas of World Water Balance, *USSR National Committee for the International Water Decade and UNESCO, 1977.*

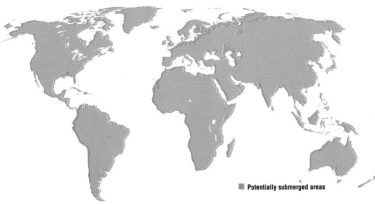

■ Potentially submerged areas

Fluctuating Sea Level

Changes in the Earth's climate have a dramatic effect on the sea level. Only 20,000 years ago, at the height of the most recent ice age, a vast amount of the Earth's water was locked up in ice sheets and glaciers, and the sea level was 330 feet (100 meters) lower than it is today. As the climate warmed slowly, the ice began to melt and the oceans began to rise.

Today there is still a tremendous amount of ice on the Earth. More than nine-tenths of it resides in the enormous ice cap which covers Antarctica. Measuring about 5.4 million square miles (14 million sq km) in surface area, the ice cap is on average one mile (1.6 km) thick but in some places is nearly three miles (4.8 km) thick. If it were to melt, the oceans would rise another 200 feet (60 m), and more than half of the world's population would have to relocate.

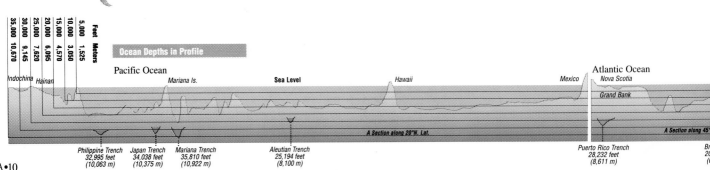

Ocean Depths in Profile

Indochina Hainan   Pacific Ocean   Mariana Is.   Sea Level   Hawaii   Mexico   Atlantic Ocean   Nova Scotia   Grand Bank

A Section along 20°N. Lat.   *A Section along 45°*

Philippine Trench 32,995 feet (10,063 m) Japan Trench 34,038 feet (10,375 m) Mariana Trench 35,810 feet (10,922 m) Aleutian Trench 25,194 feet (8,100 m)   Puerto Rico Trench 28,232 feet (8,611 m)

Deepest Lakes

Lake	Greatest depth feet	Greatest depth meters
1 Baikal, Lake, Russia	5,315	1,621
2 Tanganyika, Lake, Africa	4,800	1,464
3 Caspian Sea, Asia-Europe	3,363	1,025
4 Nyasa, Lake (Lake Malawi), Malawi-Mozambique-Tanzania	2,317	706
5 Issyk-Kul', Lake, Kyrgyzstan	2,303	702
6 Great Slave Lake, NWT, Canada	2,015	614
7 Matana, Lake, Indonesia	1,936	590
8 Crater Lake, Oregon, U.S.	1,932	589
9 Toba, Lake, Indonesia	1,736	529
10 Sarez, Lake, Tajikistan	1,657	505
11 Tahoe, Lake, California-Nevada, U.S.	1,645	502
12 Kivu, Lake, Rwanda-Zaire	1,628	496
13 Chelan, Lake, Washington, U.S.	1,605	489
14 Quesnel Lake, BC, Canada	1,560	476
15 Adams Lake, BC, Canada	1,500	457

Lakes with the Greatest Volume of Water

Lake	Volume of water cubic mi	Volume of water cubic km
1 Caspian Sea, Asia-Europe	18,900	78,200
2 Baikal, Lake, Russia	5,500	23,000
3 Tanganyika, Lake, Africa	4,500	18,900
4 Superior, Lake, Canada-U.S.	2,900	12,200
5 Nyasa, Lake (Lake Malawi), Malawi-Mozambique-Tanzania	1,900	7,725
6 Michigan, Lake, U.S.	1,200	4,910
7 Huron, Lake, Canada-U.S.	860	3,580
8 Victoria, Lake, Kenya-Tanzania-Uganda	650	2,700
9 Issyk-Kul', Lake, Kyrgyzstan	415	1,730
10 Ontario, Lake, Canada-U.S.	410	1,710
11 Great Slave Lake, Canada	260	1,070
12 Aral Sea, Kazakhstan-Uzbekistan	250	1,020
13 Great Bear Lake, Canada	240	1,010
14 Ladozhskoye, Ozero, Russia	220	908
15 Titicaca, Lake, Bolivia-Peru	170	710

Sources for volume and depth information: Atlas of World Water Balance, *USSR National Committee for the International Water Decade and UNESCO, 1977;* Principal Rivers and Lakes of the World, *National Oceanic and Atmospheric Administration, 1982.*

Principal Lakes

Lake	Area sq mi	Area sq km
1 Caspian Sea, Asia-Europe	143,240	370,990
2 Superior, Lake, Canada-U.S.	31,700	82,100
3 Victoria, Lake, Kenya-Tanzania-Uganda	26,820	69,463
4 Aral Sea, Kazakhstan-Uzbekistan	24,700	64,100
5 Huron, Lake, Canada-U.S.	23,000	60,000
6 Michigan, Lake, U.S.	22,300	57,800
7 Tanganyika, Lake, Africa	12,350	31,986
8 Baikal, Lake, Russia	12,200	31,500
9 Great Bear Lake, Canada	12,095	31,326
10 Nyasa, Lake (Lake Malawi), Malawi-Mozambique-Tanzania	11,150	28,878
11 Great Slave Lake, Canada	11,030	28,568
12 Erie, Lake, Canada-U.S.	9,910	25,667
13 Winnipeg, Lake, Canada	9,416	24,387
14 Ontario, Lake, Canada-U.S.	7,540	19,529
15 Balkhash, Lake, Kazakhstan	7,100	18,300
16 Ladozhskoye Ozero, Russia	6,833	17,700
17 Chad, Lake (Lac Tchad), Cameroon-Chad-Nigeria	6,300	16,300
18 Onezskoje, Ozero, Russia	3,753	9,720
19 Eyre, Lake, Australia	3,700	9,500
20 Titicaca, Lago, Bolivia-Peru	3,200	8,300
21 Nicaragua, Lago de, Nicaragua	3,150	8,158
22 Mai-Ndombe, Lac, Zaire	3,100	8,000
23 Athabasca, Lake, Canada	3,064	7,935
24 Reindeer Lake, Canada	2,568	6,650
25 Tônlé Sab, Boeng, Cambodia	2,500	6,500
26 Rudolf, Lake, Ethiopia-Kenya	2,473	6,405
27 Issyk-Kul', Ozero, Kyrgyzstan	2,425	6,280
28 Torrens, Lake, Australia	2,300	5,900
29 Albert, Lake, Uganda-Zaire	2,160	5,594
30 Vänern, Sweden	2,156	5,584
31 Nettilling Lake, Canada	2,140	5,542
32 Winnipegosis, Lake, Canada	2,075	5,374
33 Bangweulu, Lake, Zambia	1,930	4,999
34 Nipigon, Lake, Canada	1,872	4,848
35 Urmia, Lake, Iran	1,815	4,701
36 Manitoba, Lake, Canada	1,785	4,624
37 Woods, Lake of the, Canada-U.S.	1,727	4,472
38 Kyoga, Lake, Uganda	1,710	4,429
39 Great Salt Lake, U.S.	1,680	4,351

Lake Baikal

Russia's Great Lake

On a map of the world, Lake Baikal is easy to overlook — a thin blue crescent adrift in the vastness of Siberia. But its inconspicuousness is deceptive, for Baikal is one of the greatest bodies of fresh water on Earth.

Although lakes generally have a life span of less than one million years, Baikal has existed for perhaps as long as 25 million years, which makes it the world's oldest body of fresh water. It formed in a rift that tectonic forces had begun to tear open in the Earth's crust. As the rift grew, so did Baikal. Today the lake is 395 miles (636 km) long and an average of 30 miles (48 km) wide. Only seven lakes in the world have a greater surface area.

Baikal is the world's deepest lake. Its maximum depth is 5,315 feet (1,621 m) — slightly over a mile, and roughly equal to the greatest depth of the Grand Canyon. The lake bottom lies 4,250 feet (1,295 m) below sea level and two-and-a-third miles (3.75 km) below the peaks of the surounding mountains. The crustal rift which Baikal occupies is the planet's deepest land depression, extending to a depth of more than five-and-a-half miles (9 km). The lake sits atop at least four miles (6.4 km) of sediment, the accumulation of 25 million years.

More than 300 rivers empty into Baikal, but only one, the Angara, flows out of it. Despite having only 38% of the surface area of North America's Lake Superior, Baikal contains more water than all five of the Great Lakes combined. Its volume of 5,500 cubic miles (23,000 cubic km) is greater than that of any other freshwater lake in the world and represents approximately one-fifth of all of the Earth's unfrozen fresh water.

Caspian Sea

Lake Superior

Lake Victoria

Aral Sea

Lake Huron

Lake Michigan

Lake Tanganyika

Lake Baikal

Great Bear Lake

Lake Nyasa (Malawi)

Mediterranean Sea

France | Gibraltar | Malta | Israel

Indian Ocean

Sea Level

Sumba

Arctic Ocean

Pacific Ocean

North Pole | 65°N 65°S | South Pole

A Section along 10°N. Lat.

RIVERS

World's Longest Rivers

Rank	River	Miles	Kilometers	Rank	River	Miles	Kilometers
1	Nile, Africa	4,145	6,671	36	Amu Darya, Asia	1,578	2,540
2	Amazon-Ucayali, South America	4,000	6,400	37	Murray, Australia	1,566	2,520
3	Yangtze (Chang), Asia	3,900	6,300	38	Ganges, Asia	1,560	2,511
4	Mississippi-Missouri, North America	3,740	6,019	39	Pilcomayo, South America	1,550	2,494
5	Huang (Yellow), Asia	3,395	5,464	40	Euphrates, Asia	1,510	2,430
6	Ob'-Irtysh, Asia	3,362	5,410	41	Ural, Asia	1,509	2,428
7	Río de la Plata-Paraná, South America	3,030	4,876	42	Arkansas, North America	1,459	2,348
8	Congo (Zaïre), Africa	2,900	4,700	43	Colorado, North America (U.S.-Mexico)	1,450	2,334
9	Paraná, South America	2,800	4,500	44	Aldan, Asia	1,412	2,273
10	Amur-Ergun, Asia	2,761	4,444	45	Syr Darya, Asia	1,370	2,205
11	Amur (Heilong), Asia	2,744	4,416	46	Dnieper, Europe	1,350	2,200
12	Lena, Asia	2,700	4,400	47	Araguaia, South America	1,350	2,200
13	Mackenzie, North America	2,635	4,241	48	Cassai (Kasai), Africa	1,338	2,153
14	Mekong, Asia	2,600	4,200	49	Tarim, Asia	1,328	2,137
15	Niger, Africa	2,600	4,200	50	Kolyma, Asia	1,323	2,129
16	Yenisey, Asia	2,543	4,092	51	Orange, Africa	1,300	2,100
17	Missouri-Red Rock, North America	2,533	4,076	52	Negro, South America	1,300	2,100
18	Mississippi, North America	2,348	3,779	53	Ayeyarwady (Irrawaddy), Asia	1,300	2,100
19	Murray-Darling, Australia	2,330	3,750	54	Red, North America	1,270	2,044
20	Missouri, North America	2,315	3,726	55	Juruá, South America	1,250	2,012
21	Volga, Europe	2,194	3,531	56	Columbia, North America	1,240	2,000
22	Madeira, South America	2,013	3,240	57	Xingu, South America	1,230	1,979
23	São Francisco, South America	1,988	3,199	58	Ucayali, South America	1,220	1,963
24	Grande, Rio (Río Bravo), North America	1,885	3,034	59	Saskatchewan-Bow, North America	1,205	1,939
25	Purús, South America	1,860	2,993	60	Peace, North America	1,195	1,923
26	Indus, Asia	1,800	2,900	61	Tigris, Asia	1,180	1,899
27	Danube, Europe	1,776	2,858	62	Don, Europe	1,162	1,870
28	Brahmaputra, Asia	1,770	2,849	63	Songhua, Asia	1,140	1,835
29	Yukon, North America	1,770	2,849	64	Pechora, Europe	1,124	1,809
30	Salween (Nu), Asia	1,750	2,816	65	Kama, Europe	1,122	1,805
31	Zambezi, Africa	1,700	2,700	66	Limpopo, Africa	1,120	1,800
32	Vilyuy, Asia	1,647	2,650	67	Angara, Asia	1,105	1,779
33	Tocantins, South America	1,640	2,639	68	Snake, North America	1,038	1,670
34	Orinoco, South America	1,615	2,600	69	Uruguay, South America	1,025	1,650
35	Paraguay, South America	1,610	2,591	70	Churchill, North America	1,000	1,600

The World's Greatest River

Although the Nile is slightly longer, the Amazon surpasses all other rivers in volume, size of drainage basin, and in nearly every other important category. If any river is to be called the greatest in the world, surely it is the Amazon.

It has been estimated that one-fifth of all of the flowing water on Earth is carried by the Amazon. From its 150-mile (240-km)-wide mouth, the river discharges 6,180,000 cubic feet (174,900 cubic m) of water per second — four-and-a-half times as much as the Congo, ten times as much as the Mississippi, and fifty-six times as much as the Nile. The Amazon's tremendous outflow turns the waters of the Atlantic from salty to brackish for more than 100 miles (160 km) offshore.

Covering more than one-third of the entire continent of South America, the Amazon's vast drainage basin measures 2,669,000 square miles (6,915,000 sq km), nearly twice as large as that of the second-ranked Congo. The Amazon begins its 4,000-mile (6,400-km) journey to the Atlantic from high up in the Andes, only 100 miles (160 km) from the Pacific. Along its course it receives the waters of more than 1,000 tributaries, which rise principally from the Andes, the Guiana Highlands, and the Brazilian Highlands. Seven of the tributaries are more than 1,000 miles (1,600 km) long, and one, the Madeira, is more than 2,000 miles (3,200 km) long.

The depth of the Amazon throughout most of its Brazilian segment exceeds 150 feet (45 m). Depths of more than 300 feet (90 m) have been recorded at points near the mouth. The largest ocean-going vessels can sail as far inland as Manaus, 1,000 miles (1,600 km) from the mouth. Freighters and small passenger vessels can navigate to Iquitos, 2,300 miles (3,700 km) from the mouth, even during times of low water.

Drainage basin of the Amazon River

Rivers with the Greatest Volume of Water

Rank	River Name	Flow of water per second at mouth cubic feet	cubic meters	Rank	River Name	Flow of water per second at mouth cubic feet	cubic meters
1	Amazon, South America	6,180,000	174,900	18	Para-Tocantins, South America (joins Amazon at mouth)	360,000	10,200
2	Congo, Africa	1,377,000	39,000	19	Salween, Asia	353,000	10,000
3	Negro, South America (tributary of Amazon)	1,236,000	35,000	20	Cassai (Kasai), Africa (trib. of Congo)	351,000	9,900
4	Orinoco, South America (trib. of Amazon)	890,000	25,200	21	Mackenzie, North America	343,000	9,700
5	Río de la Plata-Paraná, South America	809,000	22,900	22	Volga, Europe	271,000	7,700
6	Yangtze (Chang), Asia;	770,000	21,800	23	Ohio, North America (trib. of Mississippi)	257,000	7,300
	Madeira, South America (trib. of Amazon)	770,000	21,800	24	Yukon, North America	240,000	6,800
7	Missouri, North America (trib. of Mississippi)	763,000	21,600	25	Indus, Asia	235,000	6,600
8	Mississippi, North America*	640,300	18,100	26	Danube, Europe	227,000	6,400
9	Yenisey, Asia	636,000	18,000	27	Niger, Africa	215,000	6,100
10	Brahmaputra, Asia	575,000	16,300	28	Atchafalaya, North America	181,000	5,100
11	Lena, Asia	569,000	16,100	29	Paraguay, South America	155,000	4,400
12	Zambesi, Africa	565,000	16,000	30	Ob'-Katun, Asia	147,000	4,200
13	Mekong, Asia	500,000	14,100	31	São Francisco, South America	120,000	3,400
14	Saint Lawrence, North America	460,000	13,000	32	Tunguska, Asia	118,000	3,350
15	Ayeyarwady (Irrawaddy), Asia	447,000	12,600	33	Huang (Yellow), Asia	116,000	3,300
16	Ob'-Irtysh, Asia; Ganges, Asia	441,000	12,500	34	Nile, Africa	110,000	3,100
17	Amur, Asia	390,000	11,000				

*Approximately one-third of the Mississippi's water is diverted above Baton Rouge, Louisiana, and reaches the Gulf of Mexico via the Atchafalaya River.

Principal Rivers of the Continents

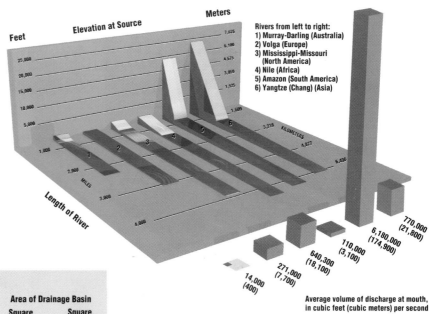

Rivers from left to right:
1) Murray-Darling (Australia)
2) Volga (Europe)
3) Mississippi-Missouri (North America)
4) Nile (Africa)
5) Amazon (South America)
6) Yangtze (Chang) (Asia)

Average volume of discharge at mouth, in cubic feet (cubic meters) per second

Rivers with the Largest Drainage Basins

Rank	River	Area of Drainage Basin Square Miles	Square Kilometers
1	Amazon, South America	2,669,000	6,915,000
2	Congo (Zaire), Africa	1,474,500	3,820,000
3	Mississippi-Missouri, North America	1,243,000	3,220,000
4	Río de la Plata-Paraná, South America	1,197,000	3,100,000
5	Ob'-Irtysh, Asia	1,154,000	2,990,000
6	Nile, Africa	1,108,000	2,870,000
7	Yenisey-Angara, Asia	1,011,000	2,618,500
8	Lena, Asia	961,000	2,490,000
9	Niger, Africa	807,000	2,090,000
10	Amur-Ergun, Asia	792,000	2,051,300
11	Yangtze (Chang), Asia	705,000	1,826,000
12	Volga, Europe	525,000	1,360,000
13	Zambesi, Africa	513,500	1,330,000
14	St. Lawrence, North America	503,000	1,302,800
15	Huang (Yellow), China	486,000	1,258,700

Sources for volume and drainage basin information: Atlas of World Water Balance, *USSR National Committee for the International Hydrological Decade and UNESCO, 1977;* Principal Rivers and Lakes of the World, *National Oceanic and Atmospheric Administration, 1982.*

CLIMATE AND WEATHER

Temperature Extremes by Continent

Africa
Highest recorded temperature
Al 'Azīzīyah, Libya, September 13, 1922:
136° F (58° C),
Lowest recorded temperature
Ifrane, Morocco, February 11, 1935:
-11° F (-24° C)

Antarctica
Highest recorded temperature
Vanda Station, January 5, 1974:
59° F (15° C)
Lowest recorded temperature
Vostok, July 21, 1983:
-129° F (-89° C)

Asia
Highest recorded temperature
Tirat Zevi, Israel, June 21, 1942:
129° F (54° C)
Lowest recorded temperature
Oymyakon and Verkhoyansk,
Russia, February 5 and 7, 1892,
and February 6, 1933: -90° F (-68° C)

Australia / Oceania
Highest recorded temperature
Cloncurry, Queensland, January 16, 1889:
128° F (53° C)
Lowest recorded temperature
Charlottes Pass, New South Wales,
June 14, 1945, and July 22, 1947: -8° F (-22° C)

Europe
Highest recorded temperature
Sevilla, Spain, August 4, 1881:
122° F (50° C)
Lowest recorded temperature
Ust' Ščugor, Russia, (date not known):
-67° F (-55° C)

North America
Highest recorded temperature
Death Valley, California, United States,
July 10, 1913: 134° F (57° C)
Lowest recorded temperature
Northice, Greenland, January 9, 1954:
-87° F (-66° C)

South America
Highest recorded temperature
Rivadavia, Argentina, December 11, 1905:
120° F (49° C)
Lowest recorded temperature
Sarmiento, Argentina, June 1, 1907:
-27° F (-33° C)

World
Highest recorded temperature
Al 'Azīzīyah, Libya, September 13, 1922:
136° F (58° C)
Lowest recorded temperature
Vostok, Antarctica, July 21, 1983:
-129° F (-89° C)

World Temperature Extremes

Highest mean annual temperature Dalol, Ethiopia, 94° F (34° C)
Lowest mean annual temperature Plateau Station, Antarctica: -70° F (-57° C)

Greatest difference between highest and lowest recorded temperatures
Verkhoyansk, Russia. The highest temperature ever recorded there is 93.5° F (34.2° C); the lowest is -89.7° F (−67.6° C)
— a difference of 183° F (102° C).

Highest temperature ever recorded at the South Pole 7.5° F (-14° C) on December 27, 1978

Most consecutive days with temperatures of 100° F (38° C) or above Marble Bar, Australia, 162 days: October 30, 1923 to April 7, 1924

Greatest rise in temperature within a 12-hour period
Granville, North Dakota, on February 21, 1918. The temperature rose 83° F (46° C), from -33° F (-36° C)
in early morning to +50° F (10° C) in late afternoon

Greatest drop in temperature within a 12-hour period
Fairfield, Montana, on December 24, 1924. The temperature dropped 84° F (46° C), from 63° F (17° C)
at noon to -21° F (-29° C) by midnight

Temperature Ranges for 14 Major Cities around the World

City	Mean Temperature Coldest Winter Month	Mean Temperature Hottest Summer Month	City	Mean Temperature Coldest Winter Month	Mean Temperature Hottest Summer Month
Bombay, India	Jan: 74.3° F (23.5° C)	May: 85.5° F (29.7° C)	Moscow, Russia	Feb: 14.5° F (-9.7° C)	Jul: 65.8° F (18.8° C)
Buenos Aires, Argentina	Aug: 51.3° F (10.7° C)	Jan: 75.0° F (23.9° C)	New York City, U.S.	Jan: 32.9° F (0.5° C)	Jul: 77.0° F (25.0° C)
Calcutta, India	Jan: 67.5° F (19.7° C)	May: 88.5° F (31.4° C)	Osaka, Japan	Jan: 40.6° F (4.8° C)	Aug: 82.2° F (27.9° C)
London, England	Feb: 39.4° F (4.1° C)	Jul: 63.9° F (17.7° C)	Rio de Janeiro, Brazil	Jul: 70.2 ° F (21.2° C)	Jan: 79.9° F (26.6° C)
Los Angeles, U.S.	Jan: 56.3° F (13.5° C)	Jul: 74.1° F (23.4° C)	São Paulo, Brazil	Jul: 58.8° F (14.9° C)	Jan: 71.1° F (21.7° C)
Manila, Philippines	Jan: 77.7° F (25.4° C)	May: 84.9° F (29.4° C)	Seoul, South Korea	Jan: 23.2° F (-4.9° C)	Aug: 77.7° F (25.4° C)
Mexico City, Mexico	Jan: 54.1° F (12.3° C)	May: 64.9° F (18.3° C)	Tokyo, Japan	Jan: 39.6° F (4.2° C)	Aug: 79.3° F (26.3° C)

Precipitation

Greatest local average annual rainfall
Mt. Waialeale, Kauai, Hawaii,
460 inches (1168 cm)

Lowest local average annual rainfall
Arica, Chile, .03 inches (.08 cm)

Greatest rainfall in 12 months
Cherrapunji, India, August 1860 to August 1861:
1,042 inches (2,647 cm)

Greatest rainfall in one month
Cherrapunji, India, July 1861: 366 inches (930 cm)

Greatest rainfall in 24 hours
Cilaos, Reunion, March 15 and 16, 1952:
74 inches (188 cm)

Greatest rainfall in 12 hours
Belouve, Reunion, February 28 and 29, 1964:
53 inches (135 cm)

Most thunderstorms annually
Kampala, Uganda averages 242 days per
year with thunderstorms

Between 1916 and 1920, Bogor, Indonesia
averaged 322 days per year with thunderstorms

Longest dry period
Arica, Chile, October, 1903
to January, 1918 — over 14 years

Largest hailstone ever recorded
Coffeyville, Kansas, U.S., September 3, 1970:
circumference 17.5 inches (44.5 cm)
diameter 5.6 inches (14 cm),
weight 1.67 pounds (758 grams)

Heaviest hailstone ever recorded
Kazakhstan, 1959: 4.18 pounds (1.9 kilograms)

North America's greatest snowfall in one season
Rainier Paradise Ranger Station, Washington,
U.S., 1971–1972: 1,122 inches (2,850 cm)

North America's greatest snowfall in one storm
Mt. Shasta Ski Bowl, California, U.S.,
February 13 to 19, 1959: 189 inches (480 cm)

North America's greatest snowfall in 24 hours
Silver Lake, Colorado, U.S., April 14 and 15, 1921:
76 inches (1 92.5 cm)

N. America's greatest depth of snowfall on the ground
Tamarack, California, U.S., March 11, 1911:
451 inches (1,145.5 cm)

Foggiest place on the U.S. West Coast
Cape Disappointment, Washington,
averages 2,552 hours of fog per year

Foggiest place on the U.S. East Coast
Mistake Island, Maine, averages
1,580 hours of fog per year

Wind

Highest 24-hour mean surface wind speed
Mt. Washington, New Hampshire, U.S.,
April 11 and 12, 1934: 128 mph (206 kph)

Highest 5-minute mean surface wind speed
Mt. Washington, New Hampshire, U.S.,
April 12, 1934: 188 mph (303 kph)

Highest surface wind peak gust:
Mt. Washington, New Hampshire, U.S.,
April 12, 1934: 231 mph (372 kph)

Windiest U.S. Cities

Chicago is sometimes called "The Windy City."
It earned this nickname because of long-winded politicians,
not because it has the strongest gales.

The windiest cities in the U.S. are as follows:

Cities	Average wind speed	
	mph	kph
Great Falls, Montana	13.1	21.0
Oklahoma City, Oklahoma	13.0	20.9
Boston, Massachusetts	12.9	20.7
Cheyenne, Wyoming	12.8	20.6
Wichita, Kansas	12.7	20.4

Chicago ranks 16th, with a 10.4 mph (16.7 kph) average.

Deadliest Hurricanes in the U.S. since 1900

Rank	Place	Year	Number of Deaths
1	Texas (Galveston)	1900	>6,000
2	Louisiana	1893	2,000
3	Florida (Lake Okeechobee)	1928	1,836
4	South Carolina, Georgia	1893	>1,000
5	Florida (Keys)	1919	>600
6	New England	1938	600
7	Florida (Keys)	1935	408
8	Southwest Louisiana, north Texas— "Hurricane Audrey"	1957	390
	Northeast U.S.	1944	390
9	Louisiana (Grand Isle)	1909	350
10	Louisana (New Orleans)	1915	275

Tornadoes in the U.S., 1950—1993

Rank	State	Total Number of Tornadoes	Yearly Average	Total Number of Deaths
1	Texas	5,303	120	471
2	Oklahoma	2,259	51	217
3	Kansas	2,068	47	199
4	Florida	1,932	44	81
5	Nebraska	1,618	37	51
U.S. Total		33,120	753	4,045

Deadliest Floods in the U.S. since 1900

Rank	Place	Year	Number of Deaths
1	Ohio River and tributaries	1913	467
2	Mississippi Valley	1927	313
3	Black Hills, South Dakota	1972	237
4	Texas rivers	1921	215
5	Northeastern U.S., following Hurricane Dianne	1955	187
6	Texas rivers	1913	177
7	James River basin, Virginia	1969	153
8	Big Thompson Canyon, Colorado	1976	139
9	Ohio and Lower Mississippi river basins	1937	137
10	Buffalo Creek, West Virginia	1972	125

POPULATION

During the first two million years of our species' existence, human population grew at a very slow rate, and probably never exceeded 10 million. With the development of agriculture circa 8000 B.C., the growth rate began to rise sharply: by the year A.D. 1, the world population stood at approximately 250 million.

By 1650 the population had doubled to 550 million, and within only 200 years it doubled again, reaching almost 1.2 billion by 1850. Each subsequent doubling has taken only about half as long as the previous one: 100 years to reach 2.5 billion, and 40 years to reach 5.2 billion.

Experts have estimated that today's world population of 5.6 billion represents 5.5% of all of the people who have ever lived on Earth.*

* Population Today, *Population Reference Bureau, February 1995*

World Population

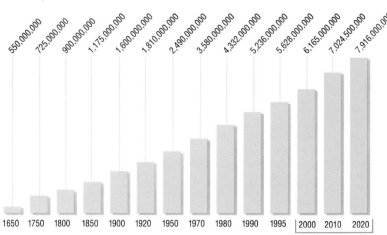

The World's Estimated Population (as of January 1, 1995): 5,628,000,000
Population Density: 97 people per square mile (37 people per square kilometer)

Historical Populations of the Continents and the World

Year	Africa	Asia	Australia	Europe	North America	Oceania, incl. Australia	South America	World
1650	*100,000,000*	335,000,000	*<1,000,000*	*100,000,000*	*5,000,000*	*2,000,000*	*8,000,000*	*550,000,000*
1750	*95,000,000*	476,000,000	*<1,000,000*	*140,000,000*	*5,000,000*	*2,000,000*	*7,000,000*	*725,000,000*
1800	*90,000,000*	593,000,000	*<1,000,000*	*190,000,000*	*13,000,000*	*2,000,000*	*12,000,000*	*900,000,000*
1850	*95,000,000*	754,000,000	*<1,000,000*	265,000,000	*39,000,000*	*2,000,000*	*20,000,000*	*1,175,000,000*
1900	118,000,000	932,000,000	4,000,000	400,000,000	106,000,000	6,000,000	38,000,000	*1,600,000,000*
1920	*140,000,000*	1,000,000,000	6,000,000	453,000,000	147,000,000	9,000,000	61,000,000	*1,810,000,000*
1950	199,000,000	1,418,000,000	8,000,000	530,000,000	219,000,000	13,000,000	111,000,000	*2,490,000,000*
1970	346,900,000	2,086,200,000	12,460,000	623,700,000	316,600,000	19,200,000	187,400,000	3,580,000,000
1980	463,800,000	2,581,000,000	14,510,000	660,000,000	365,000,000	22,700,000	239,000,000	4,332,000,000
1990	648,300,000	3,156,100,000	16,950,000	688,000,000	423,600,000	26,300,000	293,700,000	5,236,000,000

Figures for years prior to 1970 are rounded to the nearest million. Figures in italics represent rough estimates.

The 50 Most Populous Countries

Rank	Country	Population	Rank	Country	Population	Rank	Country	Population
1	China	1,196,980,000	18	United Kingdom	58,430,000	35	Algeria	27,965,000
2	India	909,150,000	19	Egypt	58,100,000	36	Morocco	26,890,000
3	United States	262,530,000	20	France	58,010,000	37	Sudan	25,840,000
4	Indonesia	193,680,000	21	Italy	57,330,000	38	Korea, North	23,265,000
5	Brazil	159,690,000	22	Ethiopia	55,070,000	39	Peru	23,095,000
6	Russia	150,500,000	23	Ukraine	52,140,000	40	Uzbekistan	22,860,000
7	Pakistan	129,630,000	24	Myanmar	44,675,000	41	Romania	22,745,000
8	Japan	125,360,000	25	Korea, South	44,655,000	42	Venezuela	21,395,000
9	Bangladesh	119,370,000	26	South Africa	44,500,000	43	Nepal	21,295,000
10	Nigeria	97,300,000	27	Zaire	43,365,000	44	Taiwan	21,150,000
11	Mexico	93,860,000	28	Spain	39,260,000	45	Iraq	20,250,000
12	Germany	81,710,000	29	Poland	38,730,000	46	Afghanistan	19,715,000
13	Vietnam	73,760,000	30	Colombia	34,870,000	47	Malaysia	19,505,000
14	Philippines	67,910,000	31	Argentina	34,083,000	48	Uganda	18,270,000
15	Iran	63,810,000	32	Kenya	28,380,000	49	Sri Lanka	18,240,000
16	Turkey	62,030,000	33	Tanzania	28,350,000	50	Australia	18,205,000
17	Thailand	59,870,000	34	Canada	28,285,000			

Most Densely Populated Countries

Rank	Country (Population)	Population per Square Mile	Population per Square Kilometer
1	Monaco (31,000)	44,286	16,316
2	Singapore (2,921,000)	11,874	4,593
3	Vatican City (1,000)	5,000	2,500
4	Malta (368,000)	3,016	1,165
5	Maldives (251,000)	2,183	842
6	Bangladesh (119,370,000)	2,147	829
7	Guernsey (64,000)	2,133	821
8	Bahrain (563,000)	2,109	815
9	Jersey (86,000)	1,911	741
10	Barbados (261,000)	1,572	607
11	Taiwan (21,150,000)	1,522	587
12	Mauritius (1,121,000)	1,423	550
13	Nauru (10,000)	1,235	476
14	Korea, South (44,655,000)	1,168	451
15	Puerto Rico (3,625,000)	1,031	398

Least Densely Populated Countries

Rank	Country (Population)	Population per Square Mile	Population per Square Kilometer
1	Greenland (57,000)	0.07	0.03
2	Mongolia (2,462,000)	4.1	1.6
3	Namibia (1,623,000)	5.1	2.0
4	Mauritania (2,228,000)	5.6	2.2
5	Australia (18,205,000)	6.1	2.4
6	Botswana (1,438,000)	6.4	2.5
7	Iceland (265,000), Suriname (426,000)	6.7	2.6
8	Canada (28,285,000)	7.3	2.8
9	Libya (5,148,000)	7.6	2.9
10	Guyana (726,000)	8.7	3.4
11	Gabon (1,035,000)	10.1	3.9
12	Chad (6,396,000)	12.9	5.0
13	Central African Republic (3,177,000)	13.0	5.1
14	Bolivia (6,790,000)	16.0	6.2
15	Kazakhstan (17,025,000)	16.3	6.3

Most Highly Urbanized Countries

Country	Urban pop. as a % of total pop.
Vatican City	100%
Singapore	100%
Monaco	100%
Belgium	96%
Kuwait	96%
San Marino	92%
Israel (excl. Occupied Areas)	92%
Venezuela	91%
Iceland	91%
Qatar	90%
Uruguay	89%
Netherlands	89%
United Kingdom	89%
Malta	87%
Argentina	86%

Least Urbanized Countries

Country	Urban pop. as a % of total pop.
Bhutan	5%
Burundi	5%
Rwanda	6%
Nepal	11%
Oman	11%
Uganda	11%
Ethiopia	12%
Cambodia (Kampuchea)	12%
Malawi	12%
Burkina Faso	15%
Eritrea	15%
Grenada	15%
Solomon Islands	15%
Bangladesh	16%
Northern Mariana Islands	16%

Fastest-Growing and Slowest-Growing Countries

A country's rate of natural increase is determined by subtracting the number of deaths from the number of births for a given period. Immigration and emigration are not included in this formulation.

The highest rate of natural increase among major countries today is Syria's 3.74%. At this rate, Syria's 1995 population of 14,100,000 will double in 19 years and triple in 30 years.

In Hungary and Ukraine deaths currently outnumber births, and the two countries share the same negative rate of natural increase, -0.026%, the lowest in the world.

When all of the countries of the world are compared, pronounced regional patterns become apparent. Of the 35 fastest-growing countries, 30 are found in either Africa or the Middle East. Of the 45 slowest-growing countries, 42 are found in Europe.

World's Largest Metropolitan Areas

Rank	Name	Population
1	Tokyo-Yokohama, Japan	30,300,000
2	New York City, U.S.	18,087,000
3	São Paulo, Brazil	16,925,000
4	Osaka-Kobe-Kyoto, Japan	16,900,000
5	Seoul, South Korea	15,850,000
6	Los Angeles, U.S.	14,531,000
7	Mexico City, Mexico	14,100,000
8	Moscow, Russia	13,150,000
9	Bombay, India	12,596,000
10	London, England	11,100,000
11	Rio de Janeiro, Brazil	11,050,000
12	Calcutta, India	11,022,000
13	Buenos Aires, Argentina	11,000,000
14	Paris, France	10,275,000
15	Jakarta, Indonesia	10,200,000

THE WORLD'S MOST POPULOUS CITIES

The following table lists the most populous cities of the world by continent and in descending order of population. It includes all cities with central city populations of 500,000 or greater. Cities with populations of less than 500,000 but with metropolitan area populations of 1,000,000 or greater have also been included in the table.

The city populations listed are the latest available census figures or official estimates. For a few cities, only unofficial estimates are available. The year in which the census was taken or to which the estimate refers is provided in parentheses preceding the city population. When comparing populations it is important to keep in mind that some figures are more current than others.

Figures in parentheses represent metropolitan area populations — the combined populations of the cities and their suburbs.

The sequence of information in each listing is as follows: city name, country name (metropolitan area population) (date of census or estimate) city population.

The Most Populous City in the World, through History

With more than 30 million people, Japan's Tokyo-Yokohama agglomeration ranks as the most populous metropolitan area in the world today. New York City held this title from the mid-1920's through the mid-1960's. But what city was the most populous in the world five hundred years ago? Five *thousand* years ago?

The following time line represents one expert's attempt to name the cities that have reigned as the most populous in the world since 3200 B.C. The time line begins with Memphis, the capital of ancient Egypt, which was possibly the first city in the world to attain a population of 20,000.

Listed after each city name is the name of the political entity to which the city belonged during the time that it was the most populous city in the world. The name of the modern political entity in which the city, its ruins, or its site is located, where this entity differs from the historic political entity, is listed in parentheses.

For the purpose of this time line, the word "city" is used in the general sense to denote a city, metropolitan area, or urban agglomeration.

It is important to note that reliable census figures are not available for most of the 5,200 years covered by this time line. Therefore the time line is somewhat subjective and conjectural.

Africa

Cairo (Al Qāhirah),
  Egypt (9,300,000) ('86) 6,068,695
Kinshasa, Zaire ('86) 3,000,000
Alexandria (Al Iskandarīyah),
  Egypt (3,350,000) ('86) 2,926,859
Casablanca (Dar-el-Beida),
  Morocco (2,475,000) ('82) 2,139,204
Abidjan, Cote d'Ivoire ('88) 1,929,079
Addis Ababa, Ethiopia (1,990,000) ('90) . 1,912,500
Giza (Al Jīzah), Egypt ('86) 1,883,189
Algiers (El Djazaïr),
  Algeria (2,547,983)('87) 1,507,241
Nairobi, Kenya ('90) 1,505,000
Dakar, Senegal ('88) 1,490,450
Luanda, Angola ('89) 1,459,900
Antananarivo, Madagascar ('88) 1,250,000
Lagos, Nigeria (3,800,000) ('87) 1,213,000
Ibadan, Nigeria ('87) 1,144,000
Dar es Salaam, Tanzania ('85) 1,096,000
Maputo, Mozambique ('89) 1,069,727
Lusaka, Zambia ('90) 982,362
Accra, Ghana (1,390,000) ('87) 949,113
Cape Town,
  South Africa (1,900,000) ('91) 854,616
Conakry, Guinea ('86) 800,000
Kampala, Uganda ('91) 773,463
Durban, South Africa (1,740,000) ('91) . . 715,669
Shubrā al Khaymah, Egypt ('86) 714,594
Johannesburg,
  South Africa (4,000,000) ('91) 712,507
Douala, Cameroon ('87) 712,251
Brazzaville, Congo ('89) 693,712
Harare, Zimbabwe (955,000) ('83) 681,000
Bamako, Mali ('87) 658,275
Wahran, Algeria ('87) 628,558
Mogadishu (Muqdisho), Somalia ('84) . . . 600,000
Bangui, Central African Republic ('89) . . . 596,800
Tunis, Tunisia (1,225,000) ('84) 596,654
Soweto, South Africa ('91) 596,632
Tripoli (Ṭarābulus),
  Libya (960,000) ('88) 591,062
Ogbomosho, Nigeria ('87) 582,900
Lubumbashi, Zaire ('84) 564,830
Yaoundé, Cameroon ('87) 560,785
Kano, Nigeria ('87) 538,300
Mombasa, Kenya ('90) 537,000
Cotonou, Benin ('92) 533,212
Omdurman (Umm Durmān),
  Sudan ('83) 526,192
Pretoria, South Africa (1,100,000) ('91) . . 525,583
Rabat, Morocco (980,000) ('82) 518,616
Lomé, Togo ('87) 500,000
N'Djamena, Chad ('88) 500,000
Khartoum (Al Khartūm),
  Sudan (1,450,000) ('83) 473,597

Asia

Seoul (Sŏul),
  South Korea (15,850,000) ('90) 10,627,790
Bombay, India (12,596,243) ('91) 9,925,891
Jakarta, Indonesia (10,200,000) ('90) . . . 8,227,746
Tōkyō, Japan (30,300,000) ('90) 8,163,573
Shanghai, China (9,300,000) ('88) 7,220,000
Delhi, India (8,419,084) ('91) 7,206,704
Beijing (Peking),
  China (7,320,000) ('88) 6,710,000
İstanbul, Turkey (7,550,000) ('90) 6,620,241
Tehrän, Iran (7,550,000) ('86) 6,042,584

Bangkok (Krung Thep),
  Thailand (7,060,000) ('91) 5,620,591
Tianjin (Tientsin), China ('88) 4,950,000
Karāchi, Pakistan (5,300,000) ('81) 4,901,627
Calcutta, India (11,021,918) ('91) 4,399,819
Shenyang (Mukden), China ('88) 3,910,000
Madras, India (5,421,985) ('91) 3,841,396
Baghdād, Iraq ('87) 3,841,268
Pusan, South Korea (3,800,000) ('90) . . . 3,797,566
Dhaka (Dacca),
  Bangladesh (6,537,308) ('91) 3,637,892
Wuhan, China ('88) 3,570,000
Yokohama, Japan ('90) 3,220,331
Guangzhou (Canton), China ('88) 3,100,000
Hyderābād, India (4,344,437) ('91) 3,043,896
Ahmadābād, India (3,312,216) ('91) 2,876,710
Thanh Pho Ho Chi Minh (Saigon),
  Vietnam (3,300,000) ('89) 2,796,229
Harbin, China ('88) 2,710,000
Lahore, Pakistan (3,025,000) ('81) 2,707,215
T'aipei, Taiwan (6,130,000) ('92) 2,706,453
Singapore, Singapore (3,025,000) ('90) . . 2,690,100
Bangalore, India (4,130,288) ('91) 2,660,088
Ōsaka, Japan (16,900,000) ('90) 2,623,801
Ankara, Turkey (2,650,000) ('90) 2,559,471
Yangon (Rangoon),
  Myanmar (2,650,000) ('83) 2,513,023
Chongqing (Chungking), China ('88) 2,502,000
Surabaya, Indonesia ('90) 2,473,272
Nanjing (Nanking), China ('88) 2,390,000
P'yŏngyang, North Korea ('81) 2,355,000
Dalian (Dairen), China ('88) 2,280,000
Taegu, South Korea ('90) 2,228,834
Xi'an (Sian), China ('88) 2,210,000
Nagoya, Japan (4,800,000) ('90) 2,154,793
Tashkent,
  Uzbekistan (2,325,000) ('91) 2,113,300
Bandung, Indonesia (2,220,000) ('90) . . . 2,058,122
Chengdu (Chengtu), China ('88) 1,884,000
Kānpur, India (2,029,889) ('91) 1,874,409
Changchun, China ('88) 1,822,000
Inch'ŏn, South Korea ('90) 1,818,293
Izmir, Turkey (1,900,000) ('90) 1,757,414
Medan, Indonesia ('90) 1,730,052
Taiyuan, China ('88) 1,700,000
Sapporo, Japan (1,900,000) ('90) 1,671,742
Quezon City, Philippines ('90) 1,666,766
Nāgpur, India (1,664,006) ('91) 1,624,752
Lucknow, India (1,669,204) ('91) 1,619,115
Manila, Philippines (9,650,000) ('90) . . . 1,598,918
Halab (Aleppo), Syria (1,640,000) ('94) . 1,591,400
Poona (Pune), India (2,493,987) ('91) . . 1,566,651
Chittagong, Bangladesh (2,342,662) ('91) 1,566,070
Damascus (Dimashq),
  Syria (2,230,000) ('94) 1,549,932
Jinan (Tsinan), China ('88) 1,546,000
New Kowloon (Xinjiulong),
  Hong Kong ('86) 1,526,910
Sürat, India (1,518,950) ('91) 1,498,817
Kōbe, Japan ('90) 1,477,410
Mashhad, Iran ('86) 1,463,508
Kyōto, Japan ('90) 1,461,103
Jaipur, India (1,518,235) ('91) 1,458,483
Novosibirsk, Russia (1,600,000) ('91) . . . 1,446,300
Kābol, Afghanistan ('88) 1,424,400
Kaohsiung, Taiwan (1,845,000) ('92) . . . 1,401,239
Anshan, China ('88) 1,330,000
Kunming, China ('88) 1,310,000
Jiddah, Saudi Arabia ('80) 1,300,000
Qingdao (Tsingtao), China ('88) 1,300,000
Lanzhou (Lanchow), China ('88) 1,297,000
Hangzhou (Hangchow), China ('88) 1,290,000

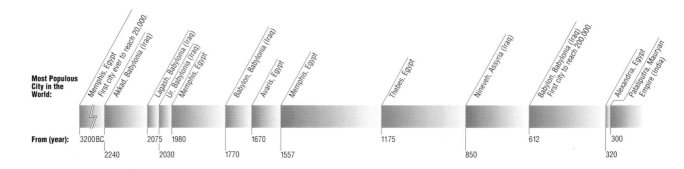

Most Populous City in the World:	Memphis, Egypt First city ever to reach 20,000.	Akkad, Babylonia (Iraq)	Lagash, Babylonia (Iraq)	Ur, Babylonia (Iraq)	Memphis, Egypt	Babylon, Babylonia (Iraq)	Avaris, Egypt	Memphis, Egypt	Thebes, Egypt	Nineveh, Assyria (Iraq)	Babylon, Babylonia (Iraq) First city to reach 200,000.	Alexandria, Egypt	Pataliputra, Mauryan Empire (India)
From (year):	3200BC.	2240	2075	1980	2030	1670	1770	1557	1175	850	612	300	320

Fushun (Funan), China ('88) 1,290,000
Tbilisi, Georgia (1,460,000) ('91) 1,279,000
Victoria, Hong Kong (4,770,000) ('91) . . 1,250,993
Riyadh (Ar-Riyād), Saudi Arabia ('80) . . . 1,250,000
Semarang, Indonesia ('90) 1,249,230
Fukuoka, Japan (1,750,000) ('90) 1,237,062
Changsha, China ('88) 1,230,000
Shijiazhuang, China ('88) 1,220,000
Jilin (Kirin), China ('88) 1,200,000
Yerevan, Armenia (1,315,000) ('89) 1,199,000
Qiqihar (Tsitsihar), China ('88) 1,180,000
Kawasaki, Japan ('90) 1,173,603
Omsk, Russia (1,190,000) ('91) 1,166,800
Alma-Ata (Almaty),
 Kazakhstan (1,190,000) ('91) 1,156,200
Zhengzhou (Chengchow), China ('88) . . . 1,150,000
Chelyabinsk, Russia (1,325,000) ('91) . . 1,148,300
Kwangju, South Korea ('90) 1,144,695
Palembang, Indonesia ('90) 1,144,047
Baotou (Paotow), China ('88) 1,130,000
Faisalabad (Lyallpur), Pakistan ('81) . . . 1,104,209
Indore, India (1,109,056) ('91) 1,091,674
Nanchang, China ('88) 1,090,000
Hiroshima, Japan (1,575,000) ('90) 1,085,705
Baku (Baki),
 Azerbaijan (2,020,000) ('91) 1,080,500
Tangshan, China ('88) 1,080,000
Bhopāl, India ('91) 1,062,771
Taejŏn, South Korea ('90) 1,062,084
Ürümqi, China ('88) 1,060,000
Ludhiāna, India ('91) 1,042,740
Vadodara, India (1,126,824) ('91) 1,031,346
Guiyang (Kweiyang), China ('88) 1,030,000
Kitakyūshū, Japan (1,525,000) ('90) . . . 1,026,455
Kalyan, India ('91) 1,014,557
Eşfahān, Iran (1,175,000) ('86) 986,753
Tabrīz, Iran ('86) 971,482
Hāora, India ('91) 950,435
Ujungpandang (Makasar), Indonesia ('90) . 944,372
Madurai, India (1,085,914) ('91) 940,989

'Ammān, Jordan (1,625,000) ('89) 936,300
Vārānasi (Benares), India (1,030,863) ('91) 929,270
Krasnoyarsk, Russia ('91) 924,400
Kuala Lumpur, Malaysia (1,475,000) ('80) . 919,610
Sendai, Japan (1,175,000) ('90) 918,398
Patna, India (1,099,647) ('91) 917,243
Adana, Turkey ('90) 916,150
Fuzhou, China ('88) 910,000
Ha Noi, Vietnam (1,275,000) ('89) 905,939
Āgra, India (948,063) ('91) 891,790
Wuxi (Wuhsi), China ('88) 880,000
Handan, China ('88) 870,000
Xuzhou (Süchow), China ('88) 860,000
Benxi (Penhsi), China ('88) 860,000
Shīrāz, Iran ('86) 848,289
Zibo (Zhangdian), China ('88) 840,000
Yichun, China ('88) 840,000
Bursa, Turkey ('90) 834,576

Chiba, Japan ('90) 829,455
Coimbatore, India (1,100,746) ('91) 816,321
Datong, China ('88) 810,000
Sakai, Japan ('90) 807,765
Thāna, India ('91) 803,369
Allahābād, India (844,546) ('91) 792,858
T'aichung, Taiwan ('92) 785,182
Kowloon (Jiulong), Hong Kong ('86) 774,781
Caloocan, Philippines ('90) 761,011
Luoyang (Loyang), China ('88) 760,000
Meerut, India (849,799) ('91) 753,778
Vishākhapatnam, India (1,057,118) ('91) . 752,037
Jabalpur, India (888,916) ('91) 741,927
Suzhou (Soochow), China ('88) 740,000
Hefei, China ('88) 740,000
Nanning, China ('88) 720,000
Jinzhou (Chinchou), China ('88) 710,000
Amritsar, India ('91) 708,835
Hyderābād, Pakistan (800,000) ('81) . . . 702,539
Vijayawāda, India (845,756) ('91) 701,827
Fuxin, China ('88) 700,000
Jixi, China ('88) 700,000
Huainan, China ('88) 700,000
Multān, Pakistan (732,070) ('81) 696,316
Malang, Indonesia ('90) 695,089
T'ainan, Taiwan ('92) 692,116
Gwalior, India (717,780) ('91) 690,765
Ulsan, South Korea ('90) 682,978
Liuzhou, China ('88) 680,000
Hohhot, China ('88) 670,000
Bucheon, South Korea ('90) 667,777
Jodhpur, India ('91) 666,279
Nāshik, India (725,341) ('91) 656,925
Mudanjiang, China ('88) 650,000
Hubli-Dhārwār, India ('91) 648,298
Vladivostok, Russia ('91) 648,000
Suwŏn, South Korea ('90) 644,968
Hims, Syria ('94) 644,204
Irkutsk, Russia ('91) 640,500
Daqing, China ('88) 640,000
Bishkek, Kyrgyzstan ('91) 631,300
Phnum Pénh, Cambodia ('90) 620,000
Xining (Sining), China ('88) 620,000
Farīdabad, India ('91) 617,717
Basra (Al Basrah), Iraq ('85) 616,700
Khabarovsk, Russia ('91) 613,300
Colombo, Sri Lanka (2,050,000) ('89) . . . 612,000
Cebu, Philippines (825,000) ('90) 610,417
Karaganda, Kazakhstan ('91) 608,600
Barnaul, Russia (673,000) ('91) 606,800
Solāpur, India (620,846) ('91) 604,215
Gaziantep, Turkey ('90) 603,434
Novokuznetsk, Russia ('91) 601,900
Khulna, Bangladesh (966,096) ('91) 601,051
Gujrānwāla, Pakistan (658,753) ('81) . . . 600,993
Rānchi, India (614,795) ('91) 599,306
Srīnagar, India (606,002) ('81) 594,775
Okayama, Japan ('90) 593,730
Hegang, China ('88) 588,300
Bareilly, India (617,350) ('91) 587,211
Guwāhāti, India ('91) 584,342
Dushanbe, Tajikistan ('91) 582,400
Ahvāz, Iran ('86) 579,826
Dandong, China ('86) 579,800
Kumamoto, Japan ('90) 579,306
Ulan Bator, Mongolia ('91) 575,000
Aurangābād, India (592,709) ('91) 573,272
Al-Mawşil, Iraq ('85) 570,926
Ningbo, China ('88) 570,000
Cochin, India (1,140,605) ('91) 564,589
Bākhtarān (Kermānshāh), Iran ('86) 560,514
Shantou (Swatow), China ('88) 560,000
Rājkot, India (654,490) ('91) 559,407

Mecca (Makkah), Saudi Arabia ('80) 550,000
Qom, Iran ('86) 543,139
Sŏngnam, South Korea ('90) 540,764
T'aipeihsien, Taiwan ('91) 538,954
Kota, India ('91) 537,371
Kagoshima, Japan ('90) 536,752
Hamamatsu, Japan ('90) 534,620
Funabashi, Japan ('90) 533,270
Mandalay, Myanmar ('83) 532,949
Sagamihara, Japan ('90) 531,542
Jerusalem (Yerushalayim) (Al-Quds),
 Israel (560,000) ('91) 524,500
Trivandrum, India (826,225) ('91) 524,006
Changzhou (Changchow), China ('86) . . . 522,700
Davao, Philippines ('90) 521,525
Kemerovo, Russia ('91) 520,700
Higashiōsaka, Japan ('90) 518,319

Chŏnju, South Korea ('90) 517,104
Pimpri-Chinchwad, India ('91) 517,083
Tsuen Wan (Quanwan), Hong Kong ('86) . . 514,241
Konya, Turkey ('90) 513,346
Jalandhar, India ('91) 509,510
Beirut (Bayrūt), Lebanon (1,675,000) ('82) 509,000
Peshāwar, Pakistan (566,248) ('81) 506,896
Tomsk, Russia ('91) 505,600
Gorakhpur, India ('91) 505,566
Chandīgarh, India (575,829) ('91) 504,094
Surakarta, Indonesia (590,000) ('90) 503,827
Zhangjiakou (Kalgan), China ('88) 500,000
Rāwalpindi, Pakistan (1,040,000) ('81) . . . 457,091
Tel Aviv-Yafo, Israel (1,735,000) ('91) . . . 339,400
Kuwait (Al-Kuwayt),
 Kuwait (1,375,000) ('85) 44,335

Australia and Oceania

Brisbane, Australia (1,334,017) ('91) 751,115
Perth, Australia (1,143,249) ('91) 80,517
Melbourne, Australia (3,022,439) ('91) 60,476
Adelaide, Australia (1,023,597) ('91) 14,843
Sydney, Australia (3,538,749) ('91) 13,501

Europe

Moscow (Moskva),
 Russia (13,150,000) ('91) 8,801,500
London, England, U.K. (11,100,000) ('81) 6,574,009
Saint Petersburg (Leningrad),
 Russia (5,525,000) ('91) 4,466,800
Berlin, Germany (4,150,000) ('91) 3,433,695
Madrid, Spain (4,650,000) ('88) 3,102,846
Rome (Roma), Italy (3,175,000) ('91) . . . 2,693,383
Kiev (Kyyiv), Ukraine (3,250,000) ('91) . . 2,635,000
Paris, France (10,275,000) ('90) 2,152,423
Bucharest (Bucureşti),
 Romania (2,300,000) ('92) 2,064,474
Budapest, Hungary (2,515,000) ('90) . . . 2,016,774
Barcelona, Spain (4,040,000) ('88) 1,714,355
Hamburg, Germany (2,385,000) ('91) . . . 1,652,363

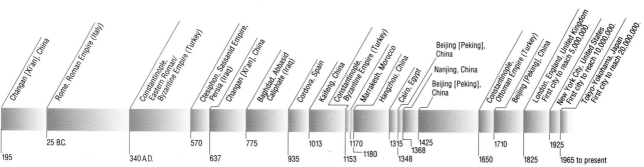

195   25 B.C.   340 A.D.   570   637   775   935   1013   1153   1170   1180   1315   1348   1368   1425   1650   1710   1825   1925   1965 to present

Changan [Xi'an], China
Rome, Roman Empire (Italy)
Constantinople, Eastern Roman/Byzantine Empire (Turkey)
Ctesiphon, Sassanid Empire, Persia (Iraq)
Changan [Xi'an], China
Baghdad, Abbasid Caliphate (Iraq)
Cordova, Spain
Kaifeng, China
Constantinople, Byzantine Empire (Turkey)
Marrakesh, Morocco
Hangzhou, China
Cairo, Egypt
Beijing [Peking], China
Nanjing, China
Beijing [Peking], China
Constantinople, Ottoman Empire (Turkey)
Beijing [Peking], China
London, England, United Kingdom
New York City, United States First city to reach 5,000,000.
First city to reach 10,000,000.
Tokyo-Yokohama, Japan First city to reach 20,000,000.

Source: Four Thousand Years of Urban Growth by Tertius Chandler, Edwin Mellen Press, 1987.

Warsaw (Warszawa), Poland (2,312,000) ('93) . . . 1,644,500
Minsk, Belarus (1,694,000) ('91) . . . 1,633,600
Kharkiv (Kharkov), Ukraine (2,050,000) ('91) . . . 1,622,800
Vienna (Wien), Austria (1,900,000) ('91) . 1,539,848
Nizhniy Novgorod (Gorky), Russia (2,025,000) ('91) . . . 1,445,000
Yekaterinburg, Russia (1,620,000) ('91) . 1,375,400
Milan (Milano), Italy (3,750,000) ('91) . . 1,371,008
Samara (Kuybyshev), Russia (1,505,000) ('91) . . . 1,257,300
Munich (München), Germany (1,900,000) ('91) . . . 1,229,026
Prague (Praha), Czech Republic (1,328,000) ('91) . . . 1,212,010
Dnipropetrovs'k, Ukraine (1,600,000) ('91) . . . 1,189,300
Sofia (Sofiya), Bulgaria (1,205,000) ('89) 1,136,875
Belgrade (Beograd), Yugoslavia (1,554,826) ('91) . . . 1,136,786
Donets'k, Ukraine (2,125,000) ('91) . . . 1,121,300
Perm', Russia (1,180,000) ('91) . . . 1,110,400
Kazan', Russia (1,165,000) ('91) . . . 1,107,300
Odesa, Ukraine (1,185,000) ('91) . . . 1,100,700
Ufa, Russia (1,118,000) ('91) . . . 1,097,000
Rostov-na-Donu, Russia (1,165,000) ('91) . . . 1,027,600
Naples (Napoli), Italy (2,875,000) ('91) . 1,024,601
Birmingham, England, U.K. (2,675,000) ('81) . . . 1,013,995
Volgograd (Stalingrad), Russia (1,360,000) ('91) . . . 1,007,300
Turin (Torino), Italy (1,550,000) ('91) . . . 961,916
Köln (Cologne), Germany (1,810,000) ('91) 953,551
Łódź, Poland (950,000) ('93) . . . 938,400
Saratov, Russia (1,155,000) ('91) . . . 911,100
Rīga, Latvia (1,005,000) ('91) . . . 910,200
Voronezh, Russia ('91) . . . 900,000
Zaporizhzhya, Ukraine ('91) . . . 896,600
Lisbon (Lisboa), Portugal (2,250,000) ('81) 807,167
L'viv (L'vov), Ukraine ('91) . . . 802,200
Marseille, France (1,225,000) ('90) . . . 800,550
Athens (Athínai), Greece (3,096,775) ('91) . 748,110
Kraków, Poland (823,000) ('93) . . . 744,000
València, Spain (1,270,000) ('88) . . . 743,933
Kryvyy Rih, Ukraine ('91) . . . 724,000
Amsterdam, Netherlands (1,875,000) ('92) . 713,407
Zagreb, Croatia ('87) . . . 697,925
Palermo, Italy ('91) . . . 697,162
Glasgow, Scotland, U.K. (1,800,000) ('90) . 689,210
Chişinău (Kishinev), Moldova ('91) . . . 676,700
Genoa (Genova), Italy (805,000) ('91) . . . 675,639
Stockholm, Sweden (1,491,726) ('91) . . . 674,452
Sevilla, Spain (945,000) ('88) . . . 663,132
Tol'yatti, Russia ('91) . . . 654,700
Ul'yanovsk, Russia ('91) . . . 648,300
Izhevsk, Russia ('91) . . . 646,800
Frankfurt (Frankfurt am Main), Germany (1,935,000) ('91) . . . 644,865
Wrocław (Breslau), Poland ('93) . . . 640,700
Yaroslavl', Russia ('91) . . . 638,100
Krasnodar, Russia ('91) . . . 631,200
Essen, Germany (5,050,000) ('91) . . . 626,973
Dortmund, Germany ('91) . . . 599,055
Vilnius, Lithuania ('92) . . . 596,900
Rotterdam, Netherlands (1,120,000) ('92) . 589,707
Poznań, Poland (666,000) ('93) . . . 582,900
Zaragoza, Spain ('88) . . . 582,239
Stuttgart, Germany (2,005,000) ('91) . . . 579,988
Düsseldorf, Germany (1,225,000) ('91) . . . 575,794
Málaga, Spain ('88) . . . 574,456
Orenburg, Russia ('91) . . . 556,500
Bremen, Germany (790,000) ('91) . . . 551,219
Penza, Russia ('91) . . . 551,100
Tula, Russia (640,000) ('91) . . . 543,600
Liverpool, England, U.K. (1,525,000) ('81) . 538,809
Duisburg, Germany ('91) . . . 535,447
Ryazan', Russia ('91) . . . 527,200
Mariupol' (Zhdanov), Ukraine ('91) . . . 521,800
Hannover, Germany (1,000,000) ('91) . . . 513,010
Astrakhan', Russia ('91) . . . 511,900
Mykolayiv, Ukraine ('91) . . . 511,600
Leipzig, Germany (720,000) ('91) . . . 511,079
Naberezhnyye Chelny, Russia ('91) . . . 510,100
Luhans'k, Ukraine (650,000) ('91) . . . 503,900
Gomel', Belarus ('91) . . . 503,300
Dublin, Ireland (1,140,000) ('86) . . . 502,749
Helsinki (Helsingfors), Finland (1,045,000) ('93) . . . 501,514
Nürnberg, Germany (1,065,000) ('91) . . . 493,692
Antwerpen, Belgium (1,140,000) ('91) . . . 467,518
Copenhagen (København), Denmark (1,670,000) ('92) . . . 464,566
Leeds, England, U.K. (1,540,000) ('81) . . . 445,242
Manchester, England, U.K. (2,775,000) ('81) . . . 437,612
Lyon, France (1,335,000) ('90) . . . 415,487
Katowice, Poland (2,770,000) ('93) . . . 359,900
Porto, Portugal (1,225,000) ('81) . . . 327,368
Mannheim, Germany (1,525,000) ('91) . . . 310,411
Newcastle upon Tyne, England, U.K. (1,300,000) ('81) . . . 199,064
Lille, France (1,050,000) ('90) . . . 172,142
Brussels (Bruxelles), Belgium (2,385,000) ('91) . . . 136,424

North America

Mexico City (Ciudad de México), Mexico (14,100,000) ('90) . . . 8,235,744
New York, N.Y., U.S. (18,087,251) ('90) . 7,322,564
Los Angeles, Ca., U.S. (14,531,529) ('90) 3,485,398
Chicago, Il., U.S. (8,065,633) ('90) . . . 2,783,726
Santo Domingo, Dominican Republic ('90) . . . 2,411,900
Havana (La Habana), Cuba (2,210,000) ('91) . . . 2,119,059
Guadalajara, Mexico (2,325,000) ('90) . . 1,650,042
Houston, Tx., U.S. (3,711,043) ('90) . . . 1,630,553
Philadelphia, Pa., U.S. (5,899,345) ('90) . 1,585,577
Nezahualcóyotl, Mexico ('90) . . . 1,255,456
Ecatepec, Mexico ('90) . . . 1,218,135
San Diego, Ca., U.S. (2,949,000) ('90) . . 1,110,549
Monterrey, Mexico (2,015,000) ('90) . . . 1,068,996
Guatemala, Guatemala (1,400,000) ('89) . 1,057,210
Detroit, Mi., U.S. (4,665,236) ('90) . . . 1,027,974
Montréal, P.Q., Canada (3,127,242) ('91) . 1,017,666
Puebla, Mexico (1,200,000) ('90) . . . 1,007,170
Dallas, Tx., U.S. (3,885,415) ('90) . . . 1,006,877
Phoenix, Az., U.S. (2,122,101) ('90) . . . 983,403
San Antonio, Tx., U.S. (1,302,099) ('90) . . 935,933
Naucalpan de Juárez, Mexico ('90) . . . 845,960
Port-au-Prince, Haiti (880,000) ('87) . . . 797,000
Ciudad Juárez, Mexico ('90) . . . 789,522
San Jose, Ca., U.S. (1,497,577) ('90) . . . 782,248
León, Mexico ('90) . . . 758,279
Baltimore, Md., U.S. (2,382,172) ('90) . . . 736,014
Indianapolis, In., U.S. (1,249,822) ('90) . . 731,327
San Francisco, Ca., U.S. (6,253,311) ('90) . 723,959
Calgary, Ab., Canada (754,033) ('91) . . . 710,677

Tlalnepantla, Mexico ('90) . . . 702,270
Tijuana, Mexico ('90) . . . 698,752
Managua, Nicaraqua ('85) . . . 682,000
Zapopan, Mexico ('90) . . . 668,323
Toronto, On., Canada (3,893,046) ('91) . . . 635,395
Jacksonville, Fl., U.S. (906,727) ('90) . . . 635,230
Columbus, Oh., U.S. (1,377,419) ('90) . . . 632,910
Milwaukee, Wi., U.S. (1,607,183) ('90) . . . 628,088
Winnipeg, Mb., Canada (652,354) ('91) . . . 616,790
Edmonton, Ab., Canada (839,924) ('91) . . . 616,741
Memphis, Tn., U.S. (981,747) ('90) . . . 610,337
Washington, D.C., U.S. (3,923,574) ('90) . . 606,900
Kingston, Jamaica (890,000) ('91) . . . 587,798
Tegucigalpa, Honduras ('88) . . . 576,661
Boston, Ma., U.S. (4,171,643) ('90) . . . 574,283
North York, On., Canada ('91) . . . 562,564
Guadalupe, Mexico ('90) . . . 535,332
Scarborough, On., Canada ('91) . . . 524,598
Mérida, Mexico ('90) . . . 523,422
Seattle, Wa., U.S. (2,559,164) ('90) . . . 516,259
Chihuahua, Mexico ('90) . . . 516,153
Acapulco de Juárez, Mexico ('90) . . . 515,374
El Paso, Tx., U.S. (1,211,300) ('90) . . . 515,342
Cleveland, Oh., U.S. (2,759,823) ('90) . . . 505,616
New Orleans, La., U.S. (1,238,816) ('90) . . 496,938
Vancouver, B.C., Canada (1,602,502) ('91) . 471,844
Denver, Co., U.S. (1,848,319) ('90) . . . 467,610
Fort Worth, Tx., U.S. (1,332,053) ('90) . . . 447,619
Portland, Or., U.S. (1,477,895) ('90) . . . 437,319
Kansas City, Mo., U.S. (1,566,280) ('90) . . 435,146
San Juan, Puerto Rico (1,877,000) ('90) . . 426,832
Saint Louis, Mo., U.S. (2,444,099) ('90) . . 396,685
Charlotte, N.C., U.S. (1,162,093) ('90) . . 395,934
Atlanta, Ga., U.S. (2,833,511) ('90) . . . 394,017
Oakland, Ca., U.S. (2,082,914) ('90) . . . 372,242
Pittsburgh, Pa., U.S. (2,242,798) ('90) . . . 369,879
Sacramento, Ca., U.S. (1,481,102) ('90) . . 369,365
Minneapolis, Mn., U.S. (2,464,124) ('90) . 368,383
Cincinnati, Oh., U.S. (1,744,124) ('90) . . . 364,040
Miami, Fl., U.S. (3,192,582) ('90) . . . 358,548
Buffalo, N.Y., U.S. (1,189,288) ('90) . . . 328,123
Tampa, Fl., U.S. (2,067,959) ('90) . . . 280,015
San José, Costa Rica (1,355,000) ('88) . . . 278,600
Newark, N.J., U.S. (1,824,321) ('90) . . . 275,221
Anaheim, Ca., U.S. (2,410,556) ('90) . . . 266,406
Norfolk, Va., U.S. (1,396,107) ('90) . . . 261,229
Rochester, N.Y., U.S. (1,002,410) ('90) . . . 231,636
Riverside, Ca., U.S. (2,588,793) ('90) . . . 226,505
Orlando, Fl., U.S. (1,072,748) ('90) . . . 164,693
Providence, R.I., U.S. (1,141,510) ('90) . . . 160,728
Salt Lake City, Ut., U.S. (1,072,227) ('90) . 159,936
Fort Lauderdale, Fl., U.S. (1,255,488) ('90) 149,377
Hartford, Ct., U.S. (1,085,837) ('90) . . . 139,739

South America

São Paulo, Brazil (16,925,000) ('91) . . . 9,393,753
Rio de Janeiro, Brazil (11,050,000) ('91) . 5,473,909
Bogotá (Santa Fe de Bogotá), Colombia (4,260,000) ('85) . . . 3,982,941
Buenos Aires, Argentina (11,000,000) ('91) . . . 2,960,976
Salvador, Brazil (2,340,000) ('91) . . . 2,070,296
Caracas, Venezuela (4,000,000) ('90) . . . 1,824,654
Belo Horizonte, Brazil (3,340,000) ('91) . 1,529,566
Brasília, Brazil ('91) . . . 1,513,470
Guayaquil, Ecuador ('90) . . . 1,508,444
Medellín, Colombia (2,095,000) ('85) . . . 1,468,089
Cali, Colombia (1,400,000) ('85) . . . 1,350,565
Recife, Brazil (2,880,000) ('91) . . . 1,296,995
Montevideo, Uruguay (1,550,000) ('85) . 1,251,647
Maracaibo, Venezuela ('90) . . . 1,249,670
Porto Alegre, Brazil (2,850,000) ('91) . . . 1,247,352
Córdoba, Argentina (1,260,000) ('91) . . . 1,148,305
San Justo, Argentina ('91) . . . 1,111,811
Quito, Ecuador (1,300,000) ('90) . . . 1,100,847
Manaus, Brazil ('91) . . . 1,005,634
Goiânia, Brazil (1,130,000) ('91) . . . 912,136
Valencia, Venezuela ('90) . . . 903,621
Barranquilla, Colombia (1,140,000) ('85) . 899,781
Rosario, Argentina (1,190,000) ('91) . . . 894,645
Curitiba, Brazil (1,815,000) ('91) . . . 841,882
Belém, Brazil (1,355,000) ('91) . . . 765,476
Campinas, Brazil (1,290,000) ('91) . . . 759,032
Fortaleza, Brazil (2,040,000) ('91) . . . 743,335
La Paz, Bolivia (1,120,000) ('92) . . . 713,378
Santa Cruz de la Sierra, Bolivia ('92) . . . 697,278
General Sarmiento (San Miguel), Argentina ('91) . . . 646,891
Morón, Argentina ('91) . . . 641,541
Barquisimeto, Venezuela ('90) . . . 625,450
Lomas de Zamora, Argentina ('91) . . . 572,769
Osasco, Brazil ('91) . . . 566,949
Nova Iguaçu, Brazil ('91) . . . 562,062
Teresina, Brazil (665,000) ('91) . . . 556,073
Maceió, Brazil ('91) . . . 554,727
São Bernardo do Campo, Brazil ('91) . . . 550,030
Guarulhos, Brazil ('91) . . . 546,417
Cartagena, Colombia ('85) . . . 531,426
La Plata, Argentina ('91) . . . 520,449
Mar del Plata, Argentina ('91) . . . 519,707
Santo André, Brazil ('91) . . . 518,272
Campo Grande, Brazil ('91) . . . 516,403
Quilmes, Argentina ('91) . . . 509,445
Asunción, Paraguay (700,000) ('92) . . . 502,426
Santos, Brazil (1,165,000) ('91) . . . 415,554
Lima, Perú (4,608,010) ('81) . . . 371,122
Santiago, Chile (4,100,000) ('82) . . . 232,667

COUNTRIES AND FLAGS

This 12-page section presents basic information about each of the world's countries, along with an illustration of each country's flag. A total of 199 countries are listed: the world's 191 fully independent countries, and 8 internally independent countries which are under the protection of other countries in matters of defense and foreign affairs. Colonies and other dependent political entities are not listed.

The categories of information provided for each country are as follows.

Flag: In many countries two or more versions of the national flag exist. For example, there is often a "civil" version which the average person flies, and a "state" version which is flown only at government buildings and government functions. A common difference between the two is the inclusion of a coat of arms on the state version. The flag versions shown here are the ones that each country has chosen to fly at the United Nations.

Country name: The short form of the English translation of the official country name.

Official name: The long form of the English translation of the official country name.

Population: The population figures listed are 1995 estimates based on U.S. census bureau figures and other available information.

Area: Figures provided represent total land area and all inland water. They are based on official data or U.N. data.

Population density: The number of people per square mile and square kilometer, calculated by dividing the country's population figure by its area figure.

Capital: The city that serves as the official seat of government. Population figures follow the capital name. These figures are based upon the latest official data.

AFGHANISTAN
Official Name: Islamic State of Afghanistan
Population: 19,715,000
Area: 251,826 sq. mi. (652,225 sq.km.)
Density: 78/sq. mi. (30/sq. km.)
Capital: Kābol (Kabul), 1,424,400

ALGERIA
Official Name: Democratic and Popular Republic of Algeria
Population: 27,965,000
Area: 919,595 sq. mi. (2,381,741 sq. km.)
Density: 30/sq. mi. (12/sq. km.)
Capital: Algiers (El Djazaïr),1,507,241

ANGUILLA
Official Name: Anguilla
Population: 7,100
Area: 35 sq. mi. (91 sq. km.)
Density: 203/sq. mi. (78/sq. km.)
Capital: The Valley, 1,042

ALBANIA
Official Name: Republic of Albania
Population: 3,394,000
Area: 11,100 sq. mi. (28,748 sq. km.)
Density: 306/sq. mi. (118/sq. km.)
Capital: Tiranë, 238,100

ANDORRA
Official Name: Principality of Andorra
Population: 59,000
Area: 175 sq. mi. (453 sq. km.)
Density: 337/sq. mi. (130/sq. km.)
Capital: Andorra, 20,437

ANTIGUA AND BARBUDA
Official Name: Antigua and Barbuda
Population: 67,000
Area: 171 sq. mi. (442 sq. km.)
Density: 392/sq. mi. (152/sq. km.)
Capital: St. John's, 24,359

ANGOLA
Official Name: Republic of Angola
Population: 10,690,000
Area: 481,354 sq. mi. (1,246,700 sq.km.)
Density: 22/sq. mi. (8.6/sq. km.)
Capital: Luanda, 1,459,900

Countries
and Flags
continued

BAHAMAS
Official Name: Commonwealth of the
Bahamas
Population: 275,000
Area: 5,382 sq. mi. (13,939 sq. km.)
Pop. Density: 51/sq. mi. (20/sq. km.)
Capital: Nassau, 141,000

BELIZE
Official Name: Belize
Population: 212,000
Area: 8,866 sq. mi. (22,963 sq. km.)
Pop. Density: 24/sq. mi. (9.2/sq. km.)
Capital: Belmopan, 5,256

ARGENTINA
Official Name: Argentine Republic
Population: 34,083,000
Area: 1,073,519 sq. mi. (2,780,400 sq. km.)
Pop. Density: 32/sq. mi. (12/sq. km.)
Capital: Buenos Aires (de facto), 2,960,976,
and Viedma (future), 40,452

BAHRAIN
Official Name: State of Bahrain
Population: 563,000
Area: 267 sq. mi. (691 sq. km.)
Pop. Density: 2,109/sq. mi. (815/sq. km.)
Capital: Al Manāmah, 82,700

BENIN
Official Name: Republic of Benin
Population: 5,433,000
Area: 43,475 sq. mi. (112,600 sq. km.)
Pop. Density: 125/sq. mi. (48/sq. km.)
Capital: Porto-Novo (designated), 164,000,
and Cotonou (de facto), 533,212

ARMENIA
Official Name: Republic of Armenia
Population: 3,794,000
Area: 11,506 sq. mi. (29,800 sq. km.)
Pop. Density: 330/sq. mi. (127/sq. km.)
Capital: Yerevan, 1,199,000

BANGLADESH
Official Name: People's Republic of
Bangladesh
Population: 119,370,000
Area: 55,598 sq. mi. (143,998 sq. km.)
Pop. Density: 2,147/sq. mi. (829/sq. km.)
Capital: Dhaka (Dacca), 3,637,892

BHUTAN
Official Name: Kingdom of Bhutan
Population: 1,758,000
Area: 17,954 sq. mi. (46,500 sq. km.)
Pop. Density: 98/sq. mi. (38/sq. km.)
Capital: Thimphu, 12,000

AUSTRALIA
Official Name: Commonwealth of Australia
Population: 18,205,000
Area: 2,966,155 sq. mi. (7,682,300 sq. km.)
Pop. Density: 6.1/sq. mi. (2.4/sq. km.)
Capital: Canberra, 276,162

BARBADOS
Official Name: Barbados
Population: 261,000
Area: 166 sq. mi. (430 sq. km.)
Pop. Density: 1,572/sq. mi. (607/sq. km.)
Capital: Bridgetown, 5,928

BOLIVIA
Official Name: Republic of Bolivia
Population: 6,790,000
Area: 424,165 sq. mi. (1,098,581 sq. km.)
Pop. Density: 16/sq. mi. (6.2/sq. km.)
Capital: La Paz (seat of government),
713,378, and Sucre (legal capital), 131,769

AUSTRIA
Official Name: Republic of Austria
Population: 7,932,000
Area: 32,377 sq. mi. (83,856 sq. km.)
Pop. Density: 245/sq. mi. (95/sq. km.)
Capital: Vienna (Wien), 1,539,848

BELARUS
Official Name: Republic of Belarus
Population: 10,425,000
Area: 80,155 sq. mi. (207,600 sq. km.)
Pop. Density: 130/sq. mi. (50/sq. km.)
Capital: Minsk, 1,633,600

BOSNIA AND HERZEGOVINA
Official Name: Republic of Bosnia and
Herzegovina
Population: 4,481,000
Area: 19,741 sq. mi. (51,129 sq. km.)
Pop. Density: 227/sq. mi. (88/sq. km.)
Capital: Sarajevo, 341,200

AZERBAIJAN
Official Name: Azerbaijani Republic
Population: 7,491,000
Area: 33,436 sq. mi. (86,600 sq. km.)
Pop. Density: 224/sq. mi. (87/sq. km.)
Capital: Baku (Bakı), 1,080,500

BELGIUM
Official Name: Kingdom of Belgium
Population: 10,075,000
Area: 11,783 sq. mi. (30,518 sq. km.)
Pop. Density: 855/sq. mi. (330/sq. km.)
Capital: Brussels (Bruxelles), 136,424

BOTSWANA
Official Name: Republic of Botswana
Population: 1,438,000
Area: 224,711 sq. mi. (582,000 sq. km.)
Pop. Density: 6.4/sq. mi. (2.5/sq. km.)
Capital: Gaborone, 133,468

BRAZIL
Official Name: Federative Republic of Brazil
Population: 159,690,000
Area: 3,286,500 sq. mi. (8,511,996 sq. km.)
Pop. Density: 49/sq. mi. (19/sq. km.)
Capital: Brasília, 1,513,470

BRUNEI
Official Name: Negara Brunei Darussalam
Population: 289,000
Area: 2,226 sq. mi. (5,765 sq. km.)
Pop. Density: 130/sq. mi. (50/sq. km.)
Capital: Bandar Seri Begawan, 22,777

BULGARIA
Official Name: Republic of Bulgaria
Population: 8,787,000
Area: 42,855 sq. mi. (110,994 sq. km.)
Pop. Density: 205/sq. mi. (79/sq. km.)
Capital: Sofia (Sofiya), 1,136,875

BURKINA FASO
Official Name: Burkina Faso
Population: 10,275,000
Area: 105,792 sq. mi. (274,000 sq. km.)
Pop. Density: 97/sq. mi. (38/sq. km.)
Capital: Ouagadougou, 441,514

BURUNDI
Official Name: Republic of Burundi
Population: 6,192,000
Area: 10,745 sq. mi. (27,830 sq. km.)
Pop. Density: 576/sq. mi. (222/sq. km.)
Capital: Bujumbura, 226,628

CAMBODIA
Official Name: Kingdom of Cambodia
Population: 9,713,000
Area: 69,898 sq. mi. (181,035 sq. km.)
Pop. Density: 139/sq. mi. (54/sq. km.)
Capital: Phnum Pénh (Phnom Penh), 620,000

CAMEROON
Official Name: Republic of Cameroon
Population: 13,330,000
Area: 183,568 sq. mi. (475,440 sq. km.)
Pop. Density: 73/sq. mi. (28/sq. km.)
Capital: Yaoundé, 560,785

CANADA
Official Name: Canada
Population: 28,285,000
Area: 3,849,674 sq. mi. (9,970,610 sq. km.)
Pop. Density: 7.3/sq. mi. (2.8/sq. km.)
Capital: Ottawa, 313,987

CAPE VERDE
Official Name: Republic of Cape Verde
Population: 429,000
Area: 1,557 sq. mi. (4,033 sq. km.)
Pop. Density: 276/sq. mi. (106/sq. km.)
Capital: Praia, 61,644

CENTRAL AFRICAN REPUBLIC
Official Name: Central African Republic
Population: 3,177,000
Area: 240,535 sq. mi. (622,984 sq. km.)
Pop. Density: 13/sq. mi. (5.1/sq. km.)
Capital: Bangui, 596,800

CHAD
Official Name: Republic of Chad
Population: 6,396,000
Area: 495,755 sq. mi. (1,284,000 sq. km.)
Pop. Density: 13/sq. mi. (5/sq. km.)
Capital: N'Djamena, 500,000

CHILE
Official Name: Republic of Chile
Population: 14,050,000
Area: 292,135 sq. mi. (756,626 sq. km.)
Pop. Density: 48/sq. mi. (19/sq. km.)
Capital: Santiago, 232,667

CHINA
Official Name: People's Republic of China
Population: 1,196,980,000
Area: 3,689,631 sq. mi. (9,556,100 sq. km.)
Pop. Density: 324/sq. mi. (125/sq. km.)
Capital: Beijing (Peking), 6,710,000

COLOMBIA
Official Name: Republic of Colombia
Population: 34,870,000
Area: 440,831 sq. mi. (1,141,748 sq. km.)
Pop. Density: 79/sq. mi. (31/sq. km.)
Capital: Bogotá, 3,982,941

COMOROS
Official Name: Federal Islamic Republic of
the Comoros
Population: 540,000
Area: 863 sq. mi. (2,235 sq. km.)
Pop. Density: 626/sq. mi. (242/sq. km.)
Capital: Moroni, 23,432

CONGO
Official Name: Republic of the Congo
Population: 2,474,000
Area: 132,047 sq. mi. (342,000 sq. km.)
Pop. Density: 19/sq. mi. (7.2/sq. km.)
Capital: Brazzaville, 693,712

COOK ISLANDS
Official Name: Cook Islands
Population: 19,000
Area: 91 sq. mi. (236 sq. km.)
Pop. Density: 209/sq. mi. (81/sq. km.)
Capital: Avarua, 10,886

COSTA RICA
Official Name: Republic of Costa Rica
Population: 3,379,000
Area: 19,730 sq. mi. (51,100 sq. km.)
Pop. Density: 171/sq. mi. (66/sq. km.)
Capital: San José, 278,600

Countries
and Flags

continued

CZECH REPUBLIC
Official Name: Czech Republic
Population: 10,430,000
Area: 30,450 sq. mi. (78,864 sq. km.)
Pop. Density: 343/sq. mi. (132/sq. km.)
Capital: Prague (Praha), 1,212,010

EGYPT
Official Name: Arab Republic of Egypt
Population: 58,100,000
Area: 386,662 sq. mi. (1,001,449 sq. km.)
Pop. Density: 150/sq. mi. (58/sq. km.)
Capital: Cairo (Al Qāhirah), 6,068,695

COTE D'IVOIRE
Official Name: Republic of Cote d'Ivoire
Population: 14,540,000
Area: 124,518 sq. mi. (322,500 sq. km.)
Pop. Density: 117/sq. mi. (45/sq. km.)
Capital: Abidjan (de facto), 1,929,079, and
  Yamoussoukro (future), 106,786

DENMARK
Official Name: Kingdom of Denmark
Population: 5,207,000
Area: 16,639 sq. mi. (43,094 sq. km.)
Pop. Density: 313 sq. mi. (121/sq. km.)
Capital: Copenhagen (København), 464,566

EL SALVADOR
Official Name: Republic of El Salvador
Population: 5,280,000
Area: 8,124 sq. mi. (21,041 sq. km.)
Pop. Density: 650/sq. mi. (251/sq. km.)
Capital: San Salvador, 462,652

CROATIA
Official Name: Republic of Croatia
Population: 4,801,000
Area: 21,829 sq. mi. (56,538 sq. km.)
Pop. Density: 220/sq. mi. (85/sq. km.)
Capital: Zagreb, 697,925

DJIBOUTI
Official Name: Republic of Djibouti
Population: 557,000
Area: 8,958 sq. mi. (23,200 sq. km.)
Pop. Density: 62/sq. mi. (24/sq. km.)
Capital: Djibouti, 329,337

EQUATORIAL GUINEA
Official Name: Republic of Equatorial Guinea
Population: 394,000
Area: 10,831 sq. mi. (28,051 sq. km.)
Pop. Density: 36/sq. mi. (14/sq. km.)
Capital: Malabo, 31,630

CUBA
Official Name: Republic of Cuba
Population: 11,560,000
Area: 42,804 sq. mi. (110,861 sq. km.)
Pop. Density: 270/sq. mi. (104/sq. km.)
Capital: Havana (La Habana), 2,119,059

DOMINICA
Official Name: Commonwealth of Dominica
Population: 89,000
Area: 305 sq. mi. (790 sq. km.)
Pop. Density: 292/sq. mi. (113/sq. km.)
Capital: Roseau, 9,348

ERITREA
Official Name: State of Eritrea
Population: 3,458,000
Area: 36,170 sq. mi. (93,679 sq. km.)
Pop. Density: 96/sq. mi. (37/sq. km.)
Capital: Asmera, 358,100

CYPRUS
Official Name: Republic of Cyprus
Population: 551,000
Area: 2,276 sq. mi. (5,896 sq. km.)
Pop. Density: 242/sq. mi. (93/sq. km.)
Capital: Nicosia (Levkosía), 48,221

DOMINICAN REPUBLIC
Official Name: Dominican Republic
Population: 7,896,000
Area: 18,704 sq. mi. (48,442 sq. km.)
Pop. Density: 422/sq. mi. (163/sq. km.)
Capital: Santo Domingo, 2,411,900

ESTONIA
Official Name: Republic of Estonia
Population: 1,515,000
Area: 17,413 sq. mi. (45,100 sq. km.)
Pop. Density: 87/sq. mi. (34/sq. km.)
Capital: Tallinn, 481,500

CYPRUS, NORTH
Official Name: Turkish Republic of
  Northern Cyprus
Population: 182,000
Area: 1,295 sq. mi. (3,355 sq. km.)
Pop. Density: 141/sq. mi. (54/sq. km.)
Capital: Nicosia (Lefkoşa), 37,400

ECUADOR
Official Name: Republic of Ecuador
Population: 11,015,000
Area: 105,037 sq. mi. (272,045 sq. km.)
Pop. Density: 105/sq. mi. (40/sq. km.)
Capital: Quito, 1,100,847

ETHIOPIA
Official Name: Ethiopia
Population: 55,070,000
Area: 446,953 sq. mi. (1,157,603 sq. km.)
Pop. Density: 123/sq. mi. (48/sq. km.)
Capital: Addis Ababa (Adis Abeba), 1,912,500

FIJI
Official Name: Republic of Fiji
Population: 775,000
Area: 7,056 sq. mi. (18,274 sq. km.)
Pop. Density: 110/sq. mi. (42/sq. km.)
Capital: Suva, 69,665

FINLAND
Official Name: Republic of Finland
Population: 5,098,000
Area: 130,559 sq. mi. (338,145 sq. km.)
Pop. Density: 39/sq. mi. (15/sq. km.)
Capital: Helsinki (Helsingfors), 501,514

FRANCE
Official Name: French Republic
Population: 58,010,000
Area: 211,208 sq. mi. (547,026 sq. km.)
Pop. Density: 275/sq. mi. (106/sq. km.)
Capital: Paris, 2,152,423

GABON
Official Name: Gabonese Republic
Population: 1,035,000
Area: 103,347 sq. mi. (267,667 sq. km.)
Pop. Density: 10/sq. mi. (3.9/sq. km.)
Capital: Libreville, 235,700

GAMBIA
Official Name: Republic of the Gambia
Population: 1,082,000
Area: 4,127 sq. mi. (10,689 sq. km.)
Pop. Density: 262/sq. mi. (101/sq. km.)
Capital: Banjul, 44,188

GEORGIA
Official Name: Republic of Georgia
Population: 5,704,000
Area: 26,911 sq. mi. (69,700 sq. km.)
Pop. Density: 212/sq. mi. (82/sq. km.)
Capital: Tbilisi, 1,279,000

GERMANY
Official Name: Federal Republic of Germany
Population: 81,710,000
Area: 137,822 sq. mi. (356,955 sq. km.)
Pop. Density: 593/sq. mi. (229/sq. km.)
Capital: Berlin (designated), 3,433,695, and
Bonn (de facto), 292,234

GHANA
Official Name: Republic of Ghana
Population: 17,210,000
Area: 92,098 sq. mi. (238,533 sq. km.)
Pop. Density: 187/sq. mi. (72/sq. km.)
Capital: Accra, 949,113

GREECE
Official Name: Hellenic Republic
Population: 10,475,000
Area: 50,949 sq. mi. (131,957 sq. km.)
Pop. Density: 206/sq. mi. (79/sq. km.)
Capital: Athens (Athínai), 748,110

GREENLAND
Official Name: Greenland
Population: 57,000
Area: 840,004 sq. mi. (2,175,600 sq. km.)
Pop. Density: 0.1/sq. mi. (0.03/sq. km.)
Capital: Godthåb (Nuuk), 12,217

GRENADA
Official Name: Grenada
Population: 92,000
Area: 133 sq. mi. (344 sq. km.)
Pop. Density: 692/sq. mi. (267/sq. km.)
Capital: St. George's, 4,439

GUATEMALA
Official Name: Republic of Guatemala
Population: 10,420,000
Area: 42,042 sq. mi. (108,889 sq. km.)
Pop. Density: 248/sq. mi. (96/sq. km.)
Capital: Guatemala, 1,057,210

GUINEA
Official Name: Republic of Guinea
Population: 6,469,000
Area: 94,926 sq. mi. (245,857 sq. km.)
Pop. Density: 68/sq. mi. (26/sq. km.)
Capital: Conakry, 800,000

GUINEA-BISSAU
Official Name: Republic of Guinea-Bissau
Population: 1,111,000
Area: 13,948 sq. mi. (36,125 sq. km.)
Pop. Density: 80/sq. mi. (31/sq. km.)
Capital: Bissau, 125,000

GUYANA
Official Name: Co-operative Republic of
Guyana
Population: 726,000
Area: 83,000 sq. mi. (214,969 sq. km.)
Pop. Density: 8.7/sq. mi. (3.4/sq. km.)
Capital: Georgetown, 78,500

HAITI
Official Name: Republic of Haiti
Population: 7,069,000
Area: 10,714 sq. mi. (27,750 sq. km.)
Pop. Density: 660/sq. mi. (255/sq. km.)
Capital: Port-au-Prince, 797,000

HONDURAS
Official Name: Republic of Honduras
Population: 5,822,000
Area: 43,277 sq. mi. (112,088 sq. km.)
Pop. Density: 135/sq. mi. (52/sq. km.)
Capital: Tegucigalpa, 576,661

HUNGARY
Official Name: Republic of Hungary
Population: 10,270,000
Area: 35,919 sq. mi. (93,030 sq. km.)
Pop. Density: 286/sq. mi. (110/sq. km.)
Capital: Budapest, 2,016,774

Countries and Flags
continued

IRELAND
Official Name: Ireland
Population: 3,546,000
Area: 27,137 sq. mi. (70,285 sq. km.)
Pop. Density: 131/sq. mi. (50/sq. km.)
Capital: Dublin (Baile Átha Cliath), 502,749

KAZAKHSTAN
Official Name: Republic of Kazakhstan
Population: 17,025,000
Area: 1,049,156 sq. mi. (2,717,300 sq. km.)
Pop. Density: 16/sq. mi. (6.3/sq. km.)
Capital: Alma-Ata (Almaty), 1,156,200, and
  Akmola (future), 286,000

ICELAND
Official Name: Republic of Iceland
Population: 265,000
Area: 39,769 sq. mi. (103,000 sq. km.)
Pop. Density: 6.7/sq. mi. (2.6/sq. km.)
Capital: Reykjavik, 100,850

ISRAEL
Official Name: State of Israel
Population: 5,059,000
Area: 8,019 sq. mi. (20,770 sq. km.)
Pop. Density: 631/sq. mi. (244/sq. km.)
Capital: Jerusalem (Yerushalayim), 524,500

KENYA
Official Name: Republic of Kenya
Population: 28,380,000
Area: 224,961 sq. mi. (582,646 sq. km.)
Pop. Density: 126/sq. mi. (49/sq. km.)
Capital: Nairobi, 1,505,000

INDIA
Official Name: Republic of India
Population: 909,150,000
Area: 1,237,062 sq. mi. (3,203,975 sq. km.)
Pop. Density: 735/sq. mi. (284/sq. km.)
Capital: New Delhi, 301,297

ITALY
Official Name: Italian Republic
Population: 57,330,000
Area: 116,324 sq. mi. (301,277 sq. km.)
Pop. Density: 493/sq. mi. (190/sq. km.)
Capital: Rome (Roma), 2,693,383

KIRIBATI
Official Name: Republic of Kiribati
Population: 79,000
Area: 313 sq. mi. (811 sq. km.)
Pop. Density: 252/sq. mi. (97/sq. km.)
Capital: Bairiki, 2,226

INDONESIA
Official Name: Republic of Indonesia
Population: 193,680,000
Area: 752,410 sq. mi. (1,948,732 sq. km.)
Pop. Density: 257/sq. mi. (99/sq. km.)
Capital: Jakarta, 8,227,746

JAMAICA
Official Name: Jamaica
Population: 2,568,000
Area: 4,244 sq. mi. (10,991 sq. km.)
Pop. Density: 605/sq. mi. (234/sq. km.)
Capital: Kingston, 587,798

KOREA, NORTH
Official Name: Democratic People's Republic
  of Korea
Population: 23,265,000
Area: 46,540 sq. mi. (120,538 sq. km.)
Pop. Density: 500/sq. mi. (193/sq. km.)
Capital: P'yŏngyang, 2,355,000

IRAN
Official Name: Islamic Republic of Iran
Population: 63,810,000
Area: 632,457 sq. mi. (1,638,057 sq. km.)
Pop. Density: 101/sq. mi. (39/sq. km.)
Capital: Tehrān, 6,042,584

JAPAN
Official Name: Japan
Population: 125,360,000
Area: 145,870 sq. mi. (377,801 sq. km.)
Pop. Density: 859/sq. mi. (332/sq. km.)
Capital: Tōkyō, 8,163,573

KOREA, SOUTH
Official Name: Republic of Korea
Population: 44,655,000
Area: 38,230 sq. mi. (99,016 sq. km.)
Pop. Density: 1,168/sq. mi. (451/sq. km.)
Capital: Seoul (Sŏul), 10,627,790

IRAQ
Official Name: Republic of Iraq
Population: 20,250,000
Area: 169,235 sq. mi. (438,317 sq. km.)
Pop. Density: 120/sq. mi. (46/sq. km.)
Capital: Baghdād, 3,841,268

JORDAN
Official Name: Hashemite Kingdom of
  Jordan
Population: 4,028,000
Area: 35,135 sq. mi. (91,000 sq. km.)
Pop. Density: 115/sq. mi. (44/sq. km.)
Capital: 'Ammān, 936,300

KUWAIT
Official Name: State of Kuwait
Population: 1,866,000
Area: 6,880 sq. mi. (17,818 sq. km.)
Pop. Density: 271/sq. mi. (105/sq. km.)
Capital: Kuwait (Al Kuwayt), 44,335

KYRGYZSTAN
Official Name: Kyrgyz Republic
Population: 4,541,000
Area: 76,641 sq. mi. (198,500 sq. km.)
Pop. Density: 59/sq. mi. (23/sq. km.)
Capital: Bishkek, 631,300

LAOS
Official Name: Lao People's Democratic
Republic
Population: 4,768,000
Area: 91,429 sq. mi. (236,800 sq. km.)
Pop. Density: 52/sq. mi. (20/sq. km.)
Capital: Viangchan (Vientiane), 377,409

LATVIA
Official Name: Republic of Latvia
Population: 2,532,000
Area: 24,595 sq. mi. (63,700 sq. km.)
Pop. Density: 103/sq. mi. (40/sq. km.)
Capital: Rīga, 910,200

LEBANON
Official Name: Republic of Lebanon
Population: 3,660,000
Area: 4,015 sq. mi. (10,400 sq. km.)
Pop. Density: 912/sq. mi. (352/sq. km.)
Capital: Beirut (Bayrūt), 509,000

LESOTHO
Official Name: Kingdom of Lesotho
Population: 1,967,000
Area: 11,720 sq. mi. (30,355 sq. km.)
Pop. Density: 168/sq. mi. (65/sq. km.)
Capital: Maseru, 109,382

LIBERIA
Official Name: Republic of Liberia
Population: 2,771,000
Area: 38,250 sq. mi. (99,067 sq. km.)
Pop. Density: 72/sq. mi. (28/sq. km.)
Capital: Monrovia, 465,000

LIBYA
Official Name: Socialist People's Libyan
Arab Jamahiriya
Population: 5,148,000
Area: 679,362 sq. mi. (1,759,540 sq. km.)
Pop. Density: 7.6/sq. mi. (2.9/sq. km.)
Capital: Tripoli (Ţarābulus), 591,062

LIECHTENSTEIN
Official Name: Principality of Liechtenstein
Population: 30,000
Area: 62 sq. mi. (160 sq. km.)
Pop. Density: 484/sq. mi. (188/sq. km.)
Capital: Vaduz, 4,887

LITHUANIA
Official Name: Republic of Lithuania
Population: 3,757,000
Area: 25,212 sq. mi. (65,300 sq. km.)
Pop. Density: 149/sq. mi. (58/sq. km.)
Capital: Vilnius, 596,900

LUXEMBOURG
Official Name: Grand Duchy of Luxembourg
Population: 396,000
Area: 998 sq. mi. (2,586 sq. km.)
Pop. Density: 397/sq. mi. (153/sq. km.)
Capital: Luxembourg, 75,377

MACEDONIA
Official Name: Republic of Macedonia
Population: 2,102,000
Area: 9,928 sq. mi. (25,713 sq. km.)
Pop. Density: 212/sq. mi. (82/sq. km.)
Capital: Skopje, 444,900

MADAGASCAR
Official Name: Republic of Madagascar
Population: 13,645,000
Area: 226,658 sq. mi. (587,041 sq. km.)
Pop. Density: 60/sq. mi. (23/sq. km.)
Capital: Antananarivo, 1,250,000

MALAWI
Official Name: Republic of Malawi
Population: 8,984,000
Area: 45,747 sq. mi. (118,484 sq. km.)
Pop. Density: 196/sq. mi. (76/sq. km.)
Capital: Lilongwe, 223,318

MALAYSIA
Official Name: Malaysia
Population: 19,505,000
Area: 127,320 sq. mi. (329,758 sq. km.)
Pop. Density: 153/sq. mi. (59/sq. km.)
Capital: Kuala Lumpur, 919,610

MALDIVES
Official Name: Republic of Maldives
Population: 251,000
Area: 115 sq. mi. (298 sq. km.)
Pop. Density: 2,183/sq. mi. (842/sq. km.)
Capital: Male', 55,130

MALI
Official Name: Republic of Mali
Population: 9,585,000
Area: 482,077 sq. mi. (1,248,574 sq. km.)
Pop. Density: 20/sq. mi. (7.7/sq. km.)
Capital: Bamako, 658,275

MALTA
Official Name: Republic of Malta
Population: 368,000
Area: 122 sq. mi. (316 sq. km.)
Pop. Density: 3,016/sq. mi. (1,165/sq. km.)
Capital: Valletta, 9,199

MARSHALL ISLANDS
Official Name: Republic of the Marshall
Islands
Population: 55,000
Area: 70 sq. mi. (181 sq. km.)
Pop. Density: 786/sq. mi. (304/sq. km.)
Capital: Majuro (island)

Countries and Flags
continued

MONACO
Official Name: Principality of Monaco
Population: 31,000
Area: 0.7 sq. mi. (1.9 sq. km.)
Pop. Density: 44,286/sq. mi. (16,316/sq. km.)
Capital: Monaco, 31,000

MAURITANIA
Official Name: Islamic Republic of Mauritania
Population: 2,228,000
Area: 395,956 sq. mi. (1,025,520 sq. km.)
Pop. Density: 5.6/sq. mi. (2.2/sq. km.)
Capital: Nouakchott, 285,000

MONGOLIA
Official Name: Mongolia
Population: 2,462,000
Area: 604,829 sq. mi. (1,566,500 sq. km.)
Pop. Density: 4.1/sq. mi. (1.6/sq. km.)
Capital: Ulan Bator (Ulaanbaatar), 575,000

MAURITIUS
Official Name: Republic of Mauritius
Population: 1,121,000
Area: 788 sq. mi. (2,040 sq. km.)
Pop. Density: 1,423/sq. mi. (550/sq. km.)
Capital: Port Louis, 141,870

MOROCCO
Official Name: Kingdom of Morocco
Population: 26,890,000
Area: 172,414 sq. mi. (446,550 sq. km.)
Pop. Density: 156/sq. mi. (60/sq. km.)
Capital: Rabat, 518,616

MEXICO
Official Name: United Mexican States
Population: 93,860,000
Area: 759,534 sq. mi. (1,967,183 sq. km.)
Pop. Density: 124/sq. mi. (48/sq. km.)
Capital: Mexico City (Ciudad de México), 8,235,744

MOZAMBIQUE
Official Name: Republic of Mozambique
Population: 17,860,000
Area: 308,642 sq. mi. (799,380 sq. km.)
Pop. Density: 58/sq. mi. (22/sq. km.)
Capital: Maputo, 1,069,727

MICRONESIA, FEDERATED STATES OF
Official Name: Federated States of Micronesia
Population: 122,000
Area: 271 sq. mi. (702 sq. km.)
Pop. Density: 450/sq. mi. (174/sq. km.)
Capital: Kolonia (de facto), 6,169, and Paliker (future)

MYANMAR
Official Name: Union of Myanmar
Population: 44,675,000
Area: 261,228 sq. mi. (676,577 sq. km.)
Pop. Density: 171/sq. mi. (66/sq. km.)
Capital: Yangon (Rangoon), 2,513,023

MOLDOVA
Official Name: Republic of Moldova
Population: 4,377,000
Area: 13,012 sq. mi. (33,700 sq. km.)
Pop. Density: 336/sq. mi. (130/sq. km.)
Capital: Chișinău (Kishinev), 676,700

NAMIBIA
Official Name: Republic of Namibia
Population: 1,623,000
Area: 318,253 sq. mi. (824,272 sq. km.)
Pop. Density: 5.1/sq. mi. (2.0/sq. km.)
Capital: Windhoek, 114,500

NAURU
Official Name: Republic of Nauru
Population: 10,000
Area: 8.1 sq. mi. (21 sq. km.)
Pop. Density: 1,235/sq. mi. (476/sq. km.)
Capital: Yaren District

NEPAL
Official Name: Kingdom of Nepal
Population: 21,295,000
Area: 56,827 sq. mi. (147,181 sq. km.)
Pop. Density: 375/sq. mi. (145/sq. km.)
Capital: Kathmandu, 421,258

NETHERLANDS
Official Name: Kingdom of the Netherlands
Population: 15,425,000
Area: 16,164 sq. mi. (41,864 sq. km.)
Pop. Density: 954/sq. mi. (368/sq. km.)
Capital: Amsterdam (designated), 713,407, and 's-Gravenhage (The Hague) (seat of government), 445,287

NEW ZEALAND
Official Name: New Zealand
Population: 3,558,000
Area: 104,454 sq. mi. (270,534 sq. km.)
Pop. Density: 34/sq. mi. (13/sq. km.)
Capital: Wellington, 150,301

NICARAGUA
Official Name: Republic of Nicaragua
Population: 4,438,000
Area: 50,054 sq. mi. (129,640 sq. km.)
Pop. Density: 89/sq. mi. (34/sq. km.)
Capital: Managua, 682,000

NIGER
Official Name: Republic of Niger
Population: 9,125,000
Area: 489,191 sq. mi. (1,267,000 sq. km.)
Pop. Density: 19/sq. mi. (7.2/sq. km.)
Capital: Niamey, 392,165

NIGERIA
Official Name: Federal Republic of Nigeria
Population: 97,300,000
Area: 356,669 sq. mi. (923,768 sq. km.)
Pop. Density: 273/sq. mi. (105/sq. km.)
Capital: Lagos (de facto),1,213,000, and
    Abuja (designated), 250,000

PALAU
Official Name: Republic of Palau
Population: 17,000
Area: 196 sq. mi. (508 sq. km.)
Pop. Density: 87/sq. mi. (33/sq. km.)
Capital: Koror (de facto), 9,018, and
    Melekeok (future)

POLAND
Official Name: Republic of Poland
Population: 38,730,000
Area: 121,196 sq. mi. (313,895 sq. km.)
Pop. Density: 320/sq. mi. (123/sq. km.)
Capital: Warsaw (Warszawa), 1,644,500

NIUE
Official Name: Niue
Population: 1,900
Area: 100 sq. mi. (259 sq. km.)
Pop. Density: 19/sq. mi. (7.3/sq. km.)
Capital: Alofi, 706

PANAMA
Official Name: Republic of Panama
Population: 2,654,000
Area: 29,157 sq. mi. (75,517 sq. km.)
Pop. Density: 91/sq. mi. (35/sq. km.)
Capital: Panamá, 411,549

PORTUGAL
Official Name: Portuguese Republic
Population: 9,907,000
Area: 35,516 sq. mi. (91,985 sq. km.)
Pop. Density: 279/sq. mi. (108/sq. km.)
Capital: Lisbon (Lisboa), 807,167

NORTHERN MARIANA ISLANDS
Official Name: Commonwealth of the
    Northern Mariana Islands
Population: 51,000
Area: 184 sq. mi. (477 sq. km.)
Pop. Density: 277/sq. mi. (107/sq. km.)
Capital: Saipan (island)

PAPUA NEW GUINEA
Official Name: Independent State of Papua
    New Guinea
Population: 4,057,000
Area: 178,704 sq. mi. (462,840 sq. km.)
Pop. Density: 23/sq. mi. (8.8/sq. km.)
Capital: Port Moresby, 193,242

PUERTO RICO
Official Name: Commonwealth of Puerto Rico
Population: 3,625,000
Area: 3,515 sq. mi. (9,104 sq. km.)
Pop. Density: 1,031/sq. mi. (398/sq. km.)
Capital: San Juan, 426,832

NORWAY
Official Name: Kingdom of Norway
Population: 4,339,000
Area: 149,412 sq. mi. (386,975 sq. km.)
Pop. Density: 29/sq. mi. (11/sq. km.)
Capital: Oslo, 470,204

PARAGUAY
Official Name: Republic of Paraguay
Population: 4,400,000
Area: 157,048 sq. mi. (406,752 sq. km.)
Pop. Density: 28/sq. mi. (11/sq. km.)
Capital: Asunción, 502,426

QATAR
Official Name: State of Qatar
Population: 519,000
Area: 4,412 sq. mi. (11,427 sq. km.)
Pop. Density: 118/sq. mi. (45/sq. km.)
Capital: Ad Dawḥah (Doha), 217,294

OMAN
Official Name: Sultanate of Oman
Population: 2,089,000
Area: 82,030 sq. mi. (212,457 sq. km.)
Pop. Density: 25/sq. mi. (9.8/sq. km.)
Capital: Masqat (Muscat), 30,000

PERU
Official Name: Republic of Peru
Population: 23,095,000
Area: 496,225 sq. mi. (1,285,216 sq. km.)
Pop. Density: 47/sq. mi. (18/sq. km.)
Capital: Lima, 371,122

ROMANIA
Official Name: Romania
Population: 22,745,000
Area: 91,699 sq. mi. (237,500 sq. km.)
Pop. Density: 248/sq. mi. (96/sq. km.)
Capital: Bucharest (Bucureşti), 2,064,474

PAKISTAN
Official Name: Islamic Republic of Pakistan
Population: 129,630,000
Area: 339,732 sq. mi. (879,902 sq. km.)
Pop. Density: 382/sq. mi. (147/sq. km.)
Capital: Islāmābād, 204,364

PHILIPPINES
Official Name: Republic of the Philippines
Population: 67,910,000
Area: 115,831 sq. mi. (300,000 sq. km.)
Pop. Density: 586/sq. mi. (226/sq. km.)
Capital: Manila, 1,598,918

RUSSIA
Official Name: Russian Federation
Population: 150,500,000
Area: 6,592,849 sq. mi. (17,075,400 sq. km.)
Pop. Density: 23/sq. mi. (8.8/sq. km.)
Capital: Moscow (Moskva), 8,801,500

Countries and Flags

continued

SAO TOME AND PRINCIPE
Official Name: Democratic Republic of Sao Tome and Principe
Population: 127,000
Area: 372 sq. mi. (964 sq. km.)
Pop. Density: 341/sq. mi. (132/sq. km.)
Capital: São Tomé, 5,245

SLOVAKIA
Official Name: Slovak Republic
Population: 5,353,000
Area: 18,933 sq. mi. (49,035 sq. km.)
Pop. Density: 283/sq. mi. (109/sq. km.)
Capital: Bratislava, 441,453

RWANDA
Official Name: Republic of Rwanda
Population: 7,343,000
Area: 10,169 sq. mi. (26,338 sq. km.)
Pop. Density: 722/sq. mi. (279/sq. km.)
Capital: Kigali, 232,733

SAUDI ARABIA
Official Name: Kingdom of Saudi Arabia
Population: 18,190,000
Area: 830,000 sq. mi. (2,149,690 sq. km.)
Pop. Density: 22/sq. mi. (8.5/sq. km.)
Capital: Riyadh (Ar Riyād), 1,250,000

SLOVENIA
Official Name: Republic of Slovenia
Population: 1,993,000
Area: 7,820 sq. mi. (20,253 sq. km.)
Pop. Density: 255/sq. mi. (98/sq. km.)
Capital: Ljubljana, 233,200

ST. KITTS AND NEVIS
Official Name: Federation of St. Kitts and Nevis
Population: 42,000
Area: 104 sq. mi. (269 sq. km.)
Pop. Density: 404/sq. mi. (156/sq. km.)
Capital: Basseterre, 14,725

SENEGAL
Official Name: Republic of Senegal
Population: 8,862,000
Area: 75,951 sq. mi. (196,712 sq. km.)
Pop. Density: 117/sq. mi. (45/sq. km.)
Capital: Dakar, 1,490,450

SOLOMON ISLANDS
Official Name: Solomon Islands
Population: 393,000
Area: 10,954 sq. mi. (28,370 sq. km.)
Pop. Density: 36/sq. mi. (14/sq. km.)
Capital: Honiara, 30,413

ST. LUCIA
Official Name: St. Lucia
Population: 138,000
Area: 238 sq. mi. (616 sq. km.)
Pop. Density: 580/sq. mi. (224/sq. km.)
Capital: Castries, 11,147

SEYCHELLES
Official Name: Republic of Seychelles
Population: 75,000
Area: 175 sq. mi. (453 sq. km.)
Pop. Density: 429/sq. mi. (166/sq. km.)
Capital: Victoria, 23,000

SOMALIA
Official Name: Somalia
Population: 7,187,000
Area: 246,201 sq. mi. (637,657 sq. km.)
Pop. Density: 29/sq. mi. (11/sq. km.)
Capital: Mogadishu (Muqdisho), 600,000

ST. VINCENT AND THE GRENADINES
Official Name: St. Vincent and the Grenadines
Population: 110,000
Area: 150 sq. mi. (388 sq. km.)
Pop. Density: 733/sq. mi. (284/sq. km.)
Capital: Kingstown, 15,466

SIERRA LEONE
Official Name: Republic of Sierra Leone
Population: 4,690,000
Area: 27,925 sq. mi. (72,325 sq. km.)
Pop. Density: 168/sq. mi. (65/sq. km.)
Capital: Freetown, 469,776

SOUTH AFRICA
Official Name: Republic of South Africa
Population: 44,500,000
Area: 471,010 sq. mi. (1,219,909 sq. km.)
Pop. Density: 94/sq. mi. (36/sq. km.)
Capital: Pretoria (administrative), 525,583, Cape Town (legislative), 854,616, and Bloemfontein (judicial), 126,867

SAN MARINO
Official Name: Republic of San Marino
Population: 24,000
Area: 24 sq. mi. (61 sq. km.)
Pop. Density: 1,000/sq. mi. (393/sq. km.)
Capital: San Marino, 2,794

SINGAPORE
Official Name: Republic of Singapore
Population: 2,921,000
Area: 246 sq. mi. (636 sq. km.)
Pop. Density: 11,874/sq. mi. (4,593/sq. km.)
Capital: Singapore, 2,921,000

SPAIN
Official Name: Kingdom of Spain
Population: 39,260,000
Area: 194,885 sq. mi. (504,750 sq. km.)
Pop. Density: 201/sq. mi. (78/sq. km.)
Capital: Madrid, 3,102,846

SRI LANKA
Official Name: Democratic Socialist Republic
of Sri Lanka
Population: 18,240,000
Area: 24,962 sq. mi. (64,652 sq. km.)
Pop. Density: 731/sq. mi. (282/sq. km.)
Capital: Colombo (designated), 612,000, and
Sri Jayawardenepura (seat of government),
108,000

SUDAN
Official Name: Republic of the Sudan
Population: 25,840,000
Area: 967,500 sq. mi. (2,505,813 sq. km.)
Pop. Density: 27/sq. mi. (10/sq. km.)
Capital: Khartoum (Al Khartum), 473,597

SURINAME
Official Name: Republic of Suriname
Population: 426,000
Area: 63,251 sq. mi. (163,820 sq. km.)
Pop. Density: 6.7/sq. mi. (2.6/sq. km.)
Capital: Paramaribo, 241,000

SWAZILAND
Official Name: Kingdom of Swaziland
Population: 889,000
Area: 6,704 sq. mi. (17,364 sq. km.)
Pop. Density: 133/sq. mi. (51/sq. km.)
Capital: Mbabane (administrative), 38,290,
and Lobamba (legislative)

SWEDEN
Official Name: Kingdom of Sweden
Population: 8,981,000
Area: 173,732 sq. mi. (449,964 sq. km.)
Pop. Density: 52/sq. mi. (20/sq. km.)
Capital: Stockholm, 674,452

SWITZERLAND
Official Name: Swiss Confederation
Population: 7,244,000
Area: 15,943 sq. mi. (41,293 sq. km.)
Pop. Density: 454/sq. mi. (175/sq. km.)
Capital: Bern (Berne), 136,338

SYRIA
Official Name: Syrian Arab Republic
Population: 14,100,000
Area: 71,498 sq. mi. (185,180 sq. km.)
Pop. Density: 197/sq. mi. (76/sq. km.)
Capital: Damascus (Dimashq), 1,549,932

TAIWAN
Official Name: Republic of China
Population: 21,150,000
Area: 13,900 sq. mi. (36,002 sq. km.)
Pop. Density: 1,522/sq. mi. (587/sq. km.)
Capital: T'aipei, 2,706,453

TAJIKISTAN
Official Name: Republic of Tajikistan
Population: 6,073,000
Area: 55,251 sq. mi. (143,100 sq. km.)
Pop. Density: 110/sq. mi. (42/sq. km.)
Capital: Dushanbe, 582,400

TANZANIA
Official Name: United Republic of Tanzania
Population: 28,350,000
Area: 341,217 sq. mi. (883,749 sq. km.)
Pop. Density: 83/sq. mi. (32/sq. km.)
Capital: Dar es Salaam (de facto), 1,096,000,
and Dodoma (legislative), 85,000

THAILAND
Official Name: Kingdom of Thailand
Population: 59,870,000
Area: 198,115 sq. mi. (513,115 sq. km.)
Pop. Density: 302/sq. mi. (117/sq. km.)
Capital: Bangkok (Krung Thep), 5,620,591

TOGO
Official Name: Republic of Togo
Population: 4,332,000
Area: 21,925 sq. mi. (56,785 sq. km.)
Pop. Density: 198/sq. mi. (76/sq. km.)
Capital: Lomé, 500,000

TONGA
Official Name: Kingdom of Tonga
Population: 110,000
Area: 288 sq. mi. (747 sq. km.)
Pop. Density: 382/sq. mi. (147/sq. km.)
Capital: Nuku'alofa, 21,265

TRINIDAD AND TOBAGO
Official Name: Republic of Trinidad and
Tobago
Population: 1,281,000
Area: 1,980 sq. mi. (5,128 sq. km.)
Pop. Density: 647/sq. mi. (250/sq. km.)
Capital: Port of Spain, 50,878

TUNISIA
Official Name: Republic of Tunisia
Population: 8,806,000
Area: 63,170 sq. mi. (163,610 sq. km.)
Pop. Density: 139/sq. mi. (54/sq. km.)
Capital: Tunis, 596,654

TURKEY
Official Name: Republic of Turkey
Population: 62,030,000
Area: 300,948 sq. mi. (779,452 sq. km.)
Pop. Density: 206/sq. mi. (80/sq. km.)
Capital: Ankara, 2,559,471

TURKMENISTAN
Official Name: Turkmenistan
Population: 4,035,000
Area: 188,456 sq. mi. (488,100 sq. km.)
Pop. Density: 21/sq. mi. (8.3/sq. km.)
Capital: Ashkhabad, 412,200

TUVALU
Official Name: Tuvalu
Population: 10,000
Area: 10 sq. mi. (26 sq. km.)
Pop. Density: 1,000/sq. mi. (385/sq. km.)
Capital: Funafuti, 2,191

Countries and Flags
continued

URUGUAY
Official Name: Oriental Republic of Uruguay
Population: 3,317,000
Area: 68,500 sq. mi. (177,414 sq. km.)
Pop. Density: 48/sq. mi. (19/sq. km.)
Capital: Montevideo, 1,251,647

WESTERN SAMOA
Official Name: Independent State of Western
 Samoa
Population: 172,000
Area: 1,093 sq. mi. (2,831 sq. km.)
Pop. Density: 157/sq. mi. (61/sq. km.)
Capital: Apia, 34,126

UGANDA
Official Name: Republic of Uganda
Population: 18,270,000
Area: 93,104 sq. mi. (241,139 sq. km.)
Pop. Density: 196/sq. mi. (76/sq. km.)
Capital: Kampala, 773,463

UZBEKISTAN
Official Name: Republic of Uzbekistan
Population: 22,860,000
Area: 172,742 sq. mi. (447,400 sq. km.)
Pop. Density: 132/sq. mi. (51/sq. km.)
Capital: Tashkent, 2,113,300

YEMEN
Official Name: Republic of Yemen
Population: 12,910,000
Area: 203,850 sq. mi. (527,968 sq. km.)
Pop. Density: 63/sq. mi. (24/sq. km.)
Capital: Sana, 427,150

UKRAINE
Official Name: Ukraine
Population: 52,140,000
Area: 233,090 sq. mi. (603,700 sq. km.)
Pop. Density: 224/sq. mi. (86/sq. km.)
Capital: Kiev (Kyyiv), 2,635,000

VANUATU
Official Name: Republic of Vanuatu
Population: 161,000
Area: 4,707 sq. mi. (12,190 sq. km.)
Pop. Density: 34/sq. mi. (13/sq. km.)
Capital: Port Vila, 18,905

YUGOSLAVIA
Official Name: Socialist Federal Republic of
 Yugoslavia
Population: 10,765,000
Area: 39,449 sq. mi. (102,173 sq. km.)
Pop. Density: 273/sq. mi. (105/sq. km.)
Capital: Belgrade (Beograd), 1,136,786

UNITED ARAB EMIRATES
Official Name: United Arab Emirates
Population: 2,855,000
Area: 32,278 sq. mi. (83,600 sq. km.)
Pop. Density: 88/sq. mi. (34/sq. km.)
Capital: Abū Ẓaby (Abu Dhabi), 242,975

VATICAN CITY
Official Name: State of the Vatican City
Population: 1,000
Area: 0.2 sq. mi. (0.4 sq. km.)
Pop. Density: 5,000/sq. mi. (2,500/sq. km.)
Capital: Vatican City, 1,000

ZAIRE
Official Name: Republic of Zaire
Population: 43,365,000
Area: 905,355 sq. mi. (2,344,858 sq. km.)
Pop. Density: 48/sq. mi. (18/sq. km.)
Capital: Kinshasa, 3,000,000

UNITED KINGDOM
Official Name: United Kingdom of Great
 Britain and Northern Ireland
Population: 58,430,000
Area: 94,249 sq. mi. (244,101 sq. km.)
Pop. Density: 620/sq. mi. (239/sq. km.)
Capital: London, 6,574,009

VENEZUELA
Official Name: Republic of Venezuela
Population: 21,395,000
Area: 352,145 sq. mi. (912,050 sq. km.)
Pop. Density: 61/sq. mi. (23/sq. km.)
Capital: Caracas, 1,822,465

ZAMBIA
Official Name: Republic of the Zambia
Population: 8,809,000
Area: 290,587 sq. mi. (752,618 sq. km.)
Pop. Density: 30/sq. mi. (12/sq. km.)
Capital: Lusaka, 982,362

UNITED STATES
Official Name: United States of America
Population: 262,530,000
Area: 3,787,425 sq. mi. (9,809,431 sq. km.)
Pop. Density: 69/sq. mi. (27/sq. km.)
Capital: Washington, D.C., 606,900

VIETNAM
Official Name: Socialist Republic of Vietnam
Population: 73,760,000
Area: 127,428 sq. mi. (330,036 sq. km.)
Pop. Density: 579/sq. mi. (223/sq. km.)
Capital: Ha Noi, 905,939

ZIMBABWE
Official Name: Republic of Zimbabwe
Population: 11,075,000
Area: 150,872 sq. mi. (390,757 sq. km.)
Pop. Density: 73/sq. mi. (28/sq. km.)
Capital: Harare (Salisbury), 681,000

Map Symbols

In a very real sense, the whole map is a symbol, representing the world or a part of it. It is a reduced representation of the earth; each of the world's features–cities rivers, etc.–is represented on the map by a symbol. Map symbols may take the form of points, such as dots or squares (often used for cities, capital cities, or points of interest), or lines (roads, railroads, rivers). Symbols may also occupy an area, showing extent of coverage (terrain, forests, deserts). They seldom look like the feature they represent and therefore must be identified and interpreted. For instance, the maps in this atlas define political units by colored tints. Neither the colors nor the boundary lines are actually found on the surface of the earth, but because countries and states are such important political components of the world, strong symbols are used to represent them. On the maps in this atlas the surface configuration of the earth is represented by hill-shading, which gives the three-dimensional impression of landforms. This terrain representation conveys a realistic and readily visualized impression of the surface. A complete legend to the right provides a key to the other symbols on the maps in this atlas.

In this atlas a "local-name" policy generally was used for naming cities and towns and all local topographic and water features. However, for a few major cities the Anglicized name was preferred and the local name given in parentheses, for instance, Moscow (Moskva), Vienna (Wien), Prague (Praha). In countries where more than one official language is used, a name is in the dominant local language. The generic parts of local names for topographic and water features are self-explanatory in many cases because of the associated map symbols or type styles.

Cultural Features

Political Boundaries

International

Secondary: State, Provincial, etc. (Second order political unit)

Disputed de jure

Cities, Towns and Villages
(Note: On maps at 1:45,000,000 and smaller the town symbols do not follow the specific population classification shown below.)

PARIS — 1,000,000 and over

Milwaukee — 250,000 to 1,000,000

Huntsville — 100,000 to 250,000

Bloomington — 25,000 to 100,000

New Meadows — 0 to 25,000

BUDAPEST — National Capitals

Springfield — Secondary Capitals

Other Cultural Features

Research Stations

Ruins

Transportation

Primary Roads

Secondary Roads

Railroads

Topographic Features

Nev. Sajama 21,463 — Peaks
Elevations are given in feet

Water Features

Lakes and Reservoirs

Fresh Water

Fresh Water: Intermittent

Salt Water

Other Water Features

Rivers

Rivers: Intermittent

Reefs

Ice Shelf

ARCTIC OCEAN

Baffin
Bay

GREENLAND
(Den.)

ALASKA
(U.S.)

Anchorage

Dawson

ICELAND

Reykjavik

Juneau

N O R T H

UNI
KING

Hudson
Bay

C A N A D A

IRELAND

Edmonton

NEWFOUNDLAND

Winnipeg

Vancouver

Montréal

St. John's

Seattle

Ottawa

A M E R I C A

Detroit

AZORES
(Port.)

PORTUGAL

San Francisco

U N I T E D   S T A T E S

Chicago

New York

GIBRALT
(U.K.)

Washington

Los Angeles

Atlanta

CANARY ISLANDS
(Sp.)

MIDWAY IS.
(U.S.)

Houston

Tropic of Cancer

New Orleans

ATLANTIC

W. SAHA

MEXICO

Gulf of Mexico

BAHAMAS

MAURITANI

HAWAIIAN ISLANDS
(U.S.)

Havana

Mexico City

Veracruz

CUBA

HAITI

DOM. REP.

PUERTO RICO (U.S.)

CAPE VERDE

SENEGAL

Dakar

BELIZE

JAMAICA

GUADELOUPE (Fr.)

GAMBIA

PACIFIC

HOND.

Caribbean

MARTINIQUE (Fr.)

GUINEA-BISSAU

GUINEA

GUAT.

BARBADOS

EL SAL.

NIC.

Sea

TRINIDAD AND TOBAGO

SIERRA LEONE

LIBERIA

COSTA
RICA

Caracas

GUYANA

VENEZUELA

Georgetown

PALMYRA
(U.S.)

PANAMA

SURINAME

Bogotá

FRENCH GUIANA

COLOMBIA

Equator

Belém

KIRIBATI

GALAPAGOS ISLANDS
(Ecua.)

Quito

ECUADOR

Manaus

Fortaleza

SOUTH

MARQUESAS IS.
(Fr.)

OCEAN

BRAZIL

Recife

PERU

AMERICA

WESTERN
SAMOA

Lima

AMERICAN
SAMOA

La Paz

BOLIVIA

Brasilia

TONGA

COOK
ISLANDS
(N.Z.)

TAHITI

Sucre

Rio de Janeiro

Tropic of Capricorn

FRENCH POLYNESIA

PARAGUAY

São Paulo

EASTER ISLAND
(Chile)

Antofagasta

Valparaíso

ARGENTINA

URUGUAY

ARCH. DE JUAN
FERNÁNDEZ
(Chile)

Santiago

Buenos
Aires

Montevideo

CHATHAM IS.
(N.Z.)

FALKLAND IS.
(U.K.)

SOUTH GEORGIA
(U.K.)

Punta Arenas

TIERRA DEL FUEGO

SOUTH SANDWICH IS.
(U.K.)

SOUTH ORKNEY IS.
(U.K.)

Antarctic Circle

SOUTH SHETLAND IS.
(U.K.)

Weddell
Sea

Scale 1:100,000,000; one inch to 1578 miles
Robinson Projection

| 0 | 400 | 800 | 1200 | 1600 | 2000 Miles |

| 0 | 600 | 1200 | 1800 | 2400 | 3000 Kilometers |

ARCTIC OCEAN

ZEMLYA FRANTSA IOSIFA

NOVAYA ZEMLYA

FINLAND

St. Petersburg

SWEDEN

EST.

LAT.

Moscow

R U S S I A

Okhotsk

BERING SEA

Sea of Okhotsk

SAKHALIN

Berlin

GERMANY

POLAND

BELARUS

Warsaw

Kiev

UKRAINE

MOLD.

CZ.

SLK.

HUNG.

ROM.

KAZAKHSTAN

Novosibirsk

Irkutsk

Ulan Bator

M O N G O L I A

A S I A

HOKKAIDŌ

Rome

ITALY

ALB.

BUL.

GREECE

Istanbul

Ankara

Black Sea

Caspian Sea

UZBEKISTAN

KYRG.

Vladivostok

HONSHŪ

Athens

TURKEY

GEO.

ARM. AZER.

TURKMENISTAN

TAJIK.

NORTH KOREA

Sea of Japan

JAPAN

MEDITERRANEAN SEA

CRETE

CYPRUS

LEB.

SYRIA

Tehran

C H I N A

Beijing

Seoul

SOUTH KOREA

Tōkyō

TUNISIA

ISRAEL

IRAQ

Baghdad

JORDAN

IRAN

AFGHANISTAN

KYŪSHŪ

Tripoli

Cairo

KUWAIT

PAKISTAN

New Delhi

NEPAL

Shanghai

P A C I F I C

LIBYA

EGYPT

QATAR

U.A.E.

Riyadh

Karachi

Tropic of Cancer

NIGER

CHAD

A F R I C A

SUDAN

SAUDI ARABIA

Mecca

OMAN

Red Sea

BNGL.

Calcutta

I N D I A

Guangzhou

HONG KONG (U.K.)

MACAO (Port.)

TAIWAN

NORTHERN MARIANA ISLANDS (U.S.)

WAKE (U.S.)

NIGERIA

CENTRAL AFRICAN REPUBLIC

CAMEROON

YEMEN

Aden

DJIBOUTI

SOCOTRA (Yem.)

Bombay

ARABIAN SEA

MYANMAR (BURMA)

Ha Noi

LAOS

HAINAN

Ha Noi

South China Sea

GUAM (U.S.)

ETHIOPIA

Addis Ababa

LAKSHADWEEP (INDIA)

Madras

Bay of Bengal

THAILAND

Yangon

Bangkok

VIETNAM

CAMBODIA

Manila

PHILIPPINES

GABON

CONGO

ZAIRE

RWANDA

BURUNDI

UGANDA

KENYA

SOMALIA

Mogadishu

MALDIVES

SRI LANKA

Colombo

Thanh Pho Ho Chi Minh

BRUNEI

PALAU

FED. STATES OF MICRONESIA

MARSHALL ISLANDS

Brazzaville

Kinshasa

TANZANIA

Nairobi

Dar es Salaam

SEYCHELLES

MALAYSIA

SINGAPORE

BORNEO

Equator

Luanda

ANGOLA

ZAMBIA

COMOROS

I N D I A N

COCOS ISLANDS (Austl.)

SUMATRA

Jakarta

I N D O N E S I A

JAVA

NEW GUINEA

PAPUA NEW GUINEA

SOLOMON ISLANDS

NAMIBIA

BOTSWANA

ZIMBABWE

MOZAMBIQUE

MADAGASCAR

Antananarivo

MAURITIUS

REUNION (Fr.)

Darwin

CORAL SEA

VANUATU

FIJI

NEW CALEDONIA (Fr.)

Tropic of Capricorn

O C E A N

A U S T R A L I A

Brisbane

Pretoria

Maputo

SWAZILAND

LESOTHO

SOUTH AFRICA

Durban

Perth

Darling

Sydney

Canberra

Auckland

NORTH I.

Cape Town

O C E A N

Melbourne

NEW ZEALAND

Wellington

TASMANIA

Hobart

SOUTH I.

ÎLES KERGUÉLEN (Fr.)

Antarctic Circle

A N T A R C T I C A

75°

60°

45°

30°

15°

0°

15°

30°

45°

60°

75°

15° 14 30° 15 45° 16 60° 17 75° 18 90° 19 105° 20 120° 21 135° 22 150° 23 165° 24 180°

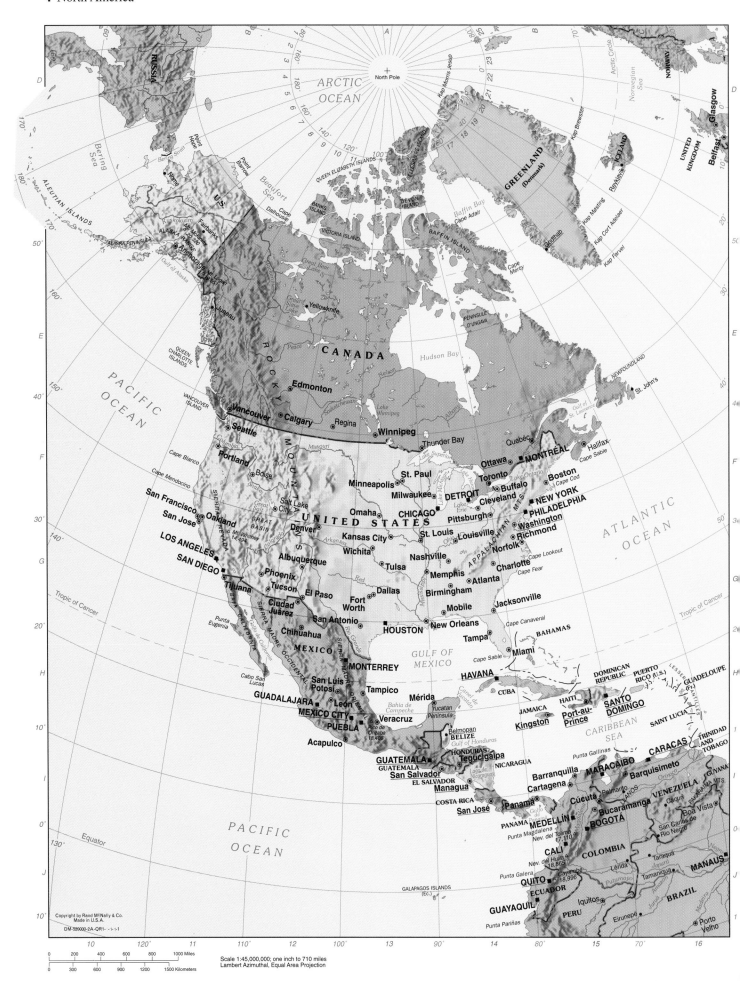

Scale 1:45,000,000; one inch to 710 miles
Lambert Azimuthal, Equal Area Projection

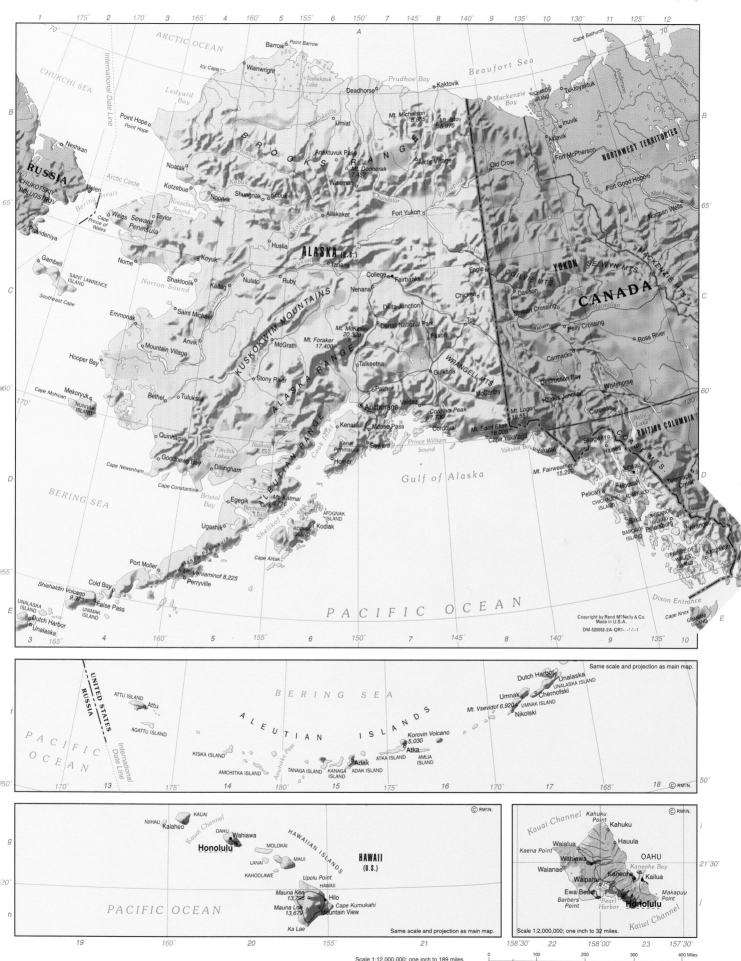

ARCTIC OCEAN

CHUKCHI SEA

Barrow • Point Barrow
Icy Cape
Wainwright •

Teshekpuk Lake
Prudhoe Bay
Kaktovik

Beaufort Sea

Cape Bathurst
Mackenzie Bay
RICHARDS ISLAND
Tuktoyaktuk
Anderson

Point Hope
Point Hope

RUSSIA
CHUKOTSKIY POLUOSTROV

Neshkan •

International Date Line

Deadhorse

Umiat

Mt. Michelson 8,855
Mt. Isto 8,975

Inuvik
NORTHWEST TERRITORIES
Aklavik
Fort McPherson

BROOKS RANGE

Noatak •
Kotzebue
Noorvik
Shungnak Kobuk

Anaktuvuk Pass
Mt. Doonerak 7,457
Wiseman

Arctic Village
Old Crow

Fort Good Hope
Norman Wells

Uelen
Bering Strait
Cape Prince of Wales

Arctic Circle

Wales
Taylor
Seward Peninsula
Kotzebue Sound

Allakaket
Chandalar

Porcupine

Eagle

Dawson
OGILVIE MTS

YUKON

SELWYN MTS.

MACKENZIE MTS.

Providenyia

Gambell
SAINT LAWRENCE ISLAND

Southeast Cape

Nome

Shaktoolik
Kaltag
Nulato
Ruby

Huslia

ALASKA (U.S.)

Tanana

College Fairbanks
Nenana

Fort Yukon

Yukon

Chicken

Stewart Crossing

Pelly Crossing

CANADA

Macmillan

Ross River

Emmonak

Saint Michael

Anvik

Mountain Village

KUSKOKWIM MOUNTAINS

McGrath

Mt. McKinley 20,320
Mt. Foraker 17,400

Delta Junction
Denali National Park

Tok
Paxon

Carmacks

Whitehorse

Pelly

BRITISH COLUMBIA

Hooper Bay

NUNIVAK ISLAND

Mekoryuk

Cape Mohican

Bethel
Tuluksak

Stony River

ALASKA RANGE

Talkeetna

Gulkana

WRANGELL MTS

McCarthy

Mt. Logan 19,551

Destruction Bay

Haines Junction

Caroross

Atlin Lake

Quinhagak
Goodnews Bay
Dillingham

Tikchik Lakes

Lake Clark

Iliamna Lake

Palmer
Anchorage Valdez
Moose Pass
Kenai

Cordova Peak 7,730
Cordova
Mt. Saint Elias 18,008
Cape Yakataga

Yakutat

Mt. Fairweather 15,299

Skagway
Haines

COAST MTS

Telegraph Creek

Cape Newenham
Cape Constantine

Bristol Bay

ALEUTIAN RANGE

Kenai Peninsula
Homer
Seward

Prince William Sound

Yakutat Bay

Pelican
CHICHAGOF ISLAND
Hoonah
ADMIRALTY ISLAND

Juneau

BERING SEA

Egegik

Becharof Lake

Mt. Katmai 6,716

Gulf of Alaska

Sitka
BARANOF ISLAND
KUPREANOF ISLAND
Petersburg

Wrangell

Ugashik

AFOGNAK ISLAND

KODIAK ISLAND
Kodiak

PRINCE OF WALES ISLAND

Ketchikan

Port Moller

ALASKA PENINSULA

Mt. Veniaminof 8,225

Cape Alitak

Dixon Entrance

Cape Knox
GRAHAM ISLAND

Shishaldin Volcano 9,373
Cold Bay
False Pass
Perryville

PACIFIC OCEAN

UNALASKA ISLAND
Dutch Harbor
Unalaska
UNIMAK ISLAND

Copyright by Rand McNally & Co.
Made in U.S.A.
DM-520552-2A-QR1- -1-1- 1

UNITED STATES
RUSSIA

ATTU ISLAND
Attu

AGATTU ISLAND

PACIFIC OCEAN

International Date Line

BERING SEA

ALEUTIAN ISLANDS

Dutch Harbor
Umnak
Chernofski
UNALASKA ISLAND
Unalaska

Mt. Vsevidof 6,920
UMNAK ISLAND
Nikolski

KISKA ISLAND

AMCHITKA ISLAND

Amchitka Pass

TANAGA ISLAND
KANAGA ISLAND
Adak
ADAK ISLAND

Korovin Volcano 5,030
ATKA ISLAND
Atka
AMLIA ISLAND

Same scale and projection as main map.

© RMcN.

NIIHAU
Kalaheo

KAUAI

OAHU
Wahiawa
Honolulu
MOLOKAI
LANAI
MAUI
KAHOOLAWE

Kauai Channel

HAWAIIAN ISLANDS

HAWAII (U.S.)

Upolu Point
HAWAII
Mauna Kea 13,796
Mauna Loa 13,679
Ka Lae

Hilo
Cape Kumukahi
Mountain View

PACIFIC OCEAN

Same scale and projection as main map.

© RMcN.

Kauai Channel

Kahuku Point
Kahuku
Hauula

Waialua
Kaena Point
Wahiawa
Waianae
Waipahu
Ewa Beach
Barbers Point
Pearl Harbor

OAHU

Kaneohe Bay
Kaneohe
Kailua

Makapuu Point

Honolulu

Kaiwi Channel

Scale 1:2,000,000; one inch to 32 miles.

Scale 1:12,000,000; one inch to 189 miles
Alber's Conic Equal Area Projection

0 100 200 300 400 Miles
0 100 200 300 400 500 600 Kilometers

Scale 1:16,000,000; one inch to 252 miles
Lambert Conformal Conic Projection

Scale 1:12,000,000; one inch to 189 miles
Alber's Conic Equal Area Projection

0   100   200   300   400 Miles

0   100   200   300   400   500   600 Kilometers

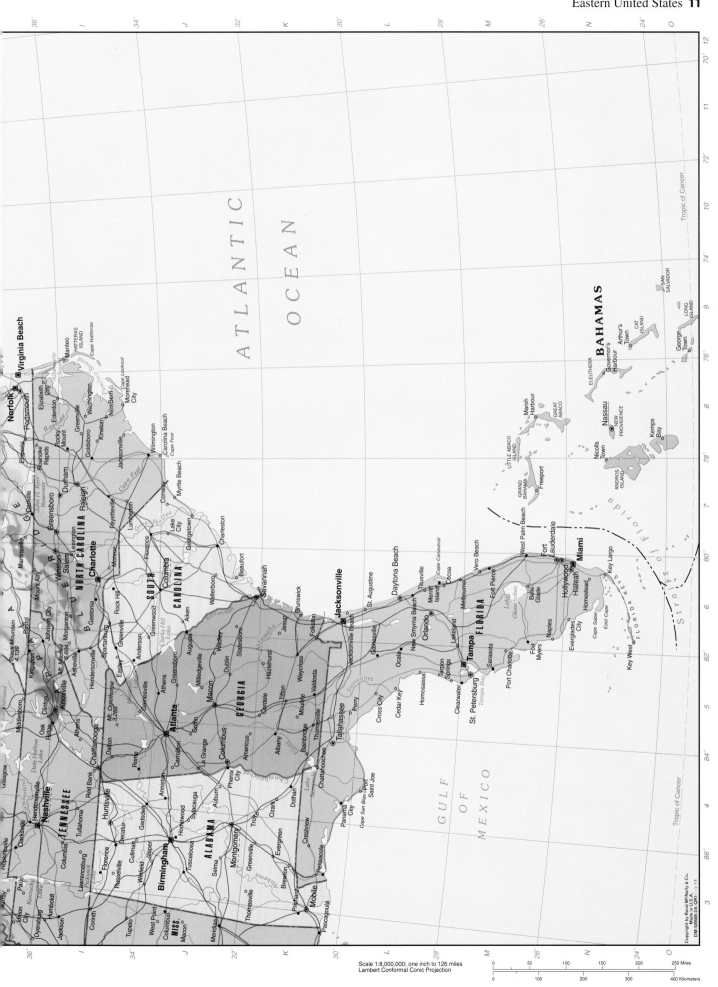

ATLANTIC

OCEAN

BAHAMAS

ELEUTHERA

SAN
SALVADOR

George
Town

LONG
ISLAND

CAT
ISLAND

Arthur's
Town

Governor's
Harbour

Kemps
Bay

NEW
PROVIDENCE

Nassau

Nicolls
Town

Marsh
Harbour

GREAT
ABACO

LITTLE ABACO
ISLAND

ANDROS
ISLAND

GRAND
BAHAMA

Freeport

Virginia Beach

Norfolk
Portsmouth

Emporia

Roanoke
Rapids

Manteo

HATTERAS
ISLAND

Cape Hatteras

Albemarle Sound

Edenton

Elizabeth
City

Pamlico Sound

Cape Lookout

Morehead
City

New Bern

Washington

Greenville

Kinston

Goldsboro

Wilmington

Carolina Beach

Cape Fear

Martinsville

Danville

Roanoke

Durham

Greensboro

Winston-
Salem

Mount Airy

NORTH CAROLINA

Raleigh

Fayetteville

Lumberton

Charlotte

Monroe

Myrtle Beach

Conway

Cape Fear

John H. Kerr
Reservoir

Black Mountain
4,139

Bristol

Johnson City

Kingsport

Mt. Mitchell
6,684

Asheville

Hendersonville

Morganton

Gastonia

Rock Hill

Spartanburg

Greenville

Easley

Anderson

SOUTH
CAROLINA

Columbia

Florence

Great Pee Dee

Lake
City

Georgetown

Charleston

Beaufort

Clarks Hill
Lake

Greenwood

Aiken

Augusta

Walterboro

Savannah

Savannah

Brunswick

Jesup

Waycross

Folkston

Jacksonville

St. Augustine

Jacksonville
Beach

Middlesboro

Knoxville

Athens

Oak
Ridge

Dale Hollow
Lake

Clinton

Red Bank

Chattanooga

Dalton

Rome

Carrollton

Mt. Oglethorpe
3,288

Gainesville

Athens

Greensboro

Milledgeville

Atlanta

Griffin

GEORGIA

Macon

Dublin

Statesboro

Hazlehurst

Wadley

Sandersville

Columbus

La Grange

Americus

Cordele

Tifton

Moultrie

Valdosta

Perry

Thomasville

Tallahassee

Bainbridge

Chattahoochee

Albany

Dothan

Daytona Beach

Thusville

Merritt
Island

Cape Canaveral

Cocoa

New Smyrna Beach

Orlando

Melbourne

Vero Beach

Fort Pierce

West Palm Beach

Fort
Lauderdale

Miami

Hollywood

Hialeah

Homestead

Key Largo

Belle
Glade

Lake
Okeechobee

FLORIDA

Naples

Everglades
City

Cape Sable

East Cape

Key West

FLORIDA KEYS

Straits of Florida

Lakeland

Tampa

St. Petersburg

Tampa Bay

Clearwater

Tarpon
Springs

Sarasota

Port Charlotte

Fort
Myers

Bradenton

Cross City

Cedar Key

Ocala

Gainesville

Homosassa

Suwannee

Panama
City

Cape San Blas

Port
Saint Joe

Crestview

Ozark

Troy

Brewton

Evergreen

Greenville

Pensacola

Mobile

Prichard

Pascagoula

GULF

OF

MEXICO

Nashville

Clarksville

Hendersonville

Murfreesboro

Tullahoma

TENNESSEE

Huntsville

Decatur

Gadsden

Homewood

Sylacauga

Birmingham

Bessemer

Tuscaloosa

Jasper

Cullman

Florence

Russellville

Winfield

ALABAMA

Montgomery

Selma

Auburn

Phenix
City

Opelika

Alabama

MISS.

Columbus

Macon

Meridian

West Point

Tupelo

Corinth

Jackson

Humboldt

Union
City

Dyersburg

Paris

Glasgow

Kentucky
Lake

Cumberland

Lawrenceburg

Columbia

Pulaski

Scale 1:8,000,000; one inch to 126 miles
Lambert Conformal Conic Projection

0   50   100   150   200   250 Miles

0   100   200   300   400 Kilometers

Tropic of Cancer

Tropic of Cancer

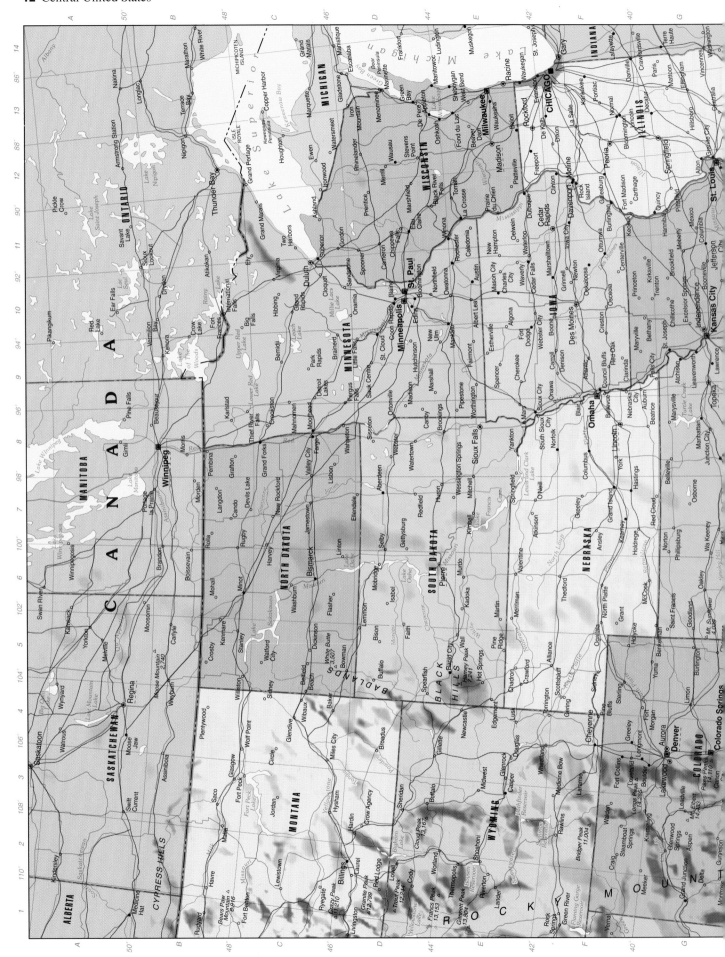

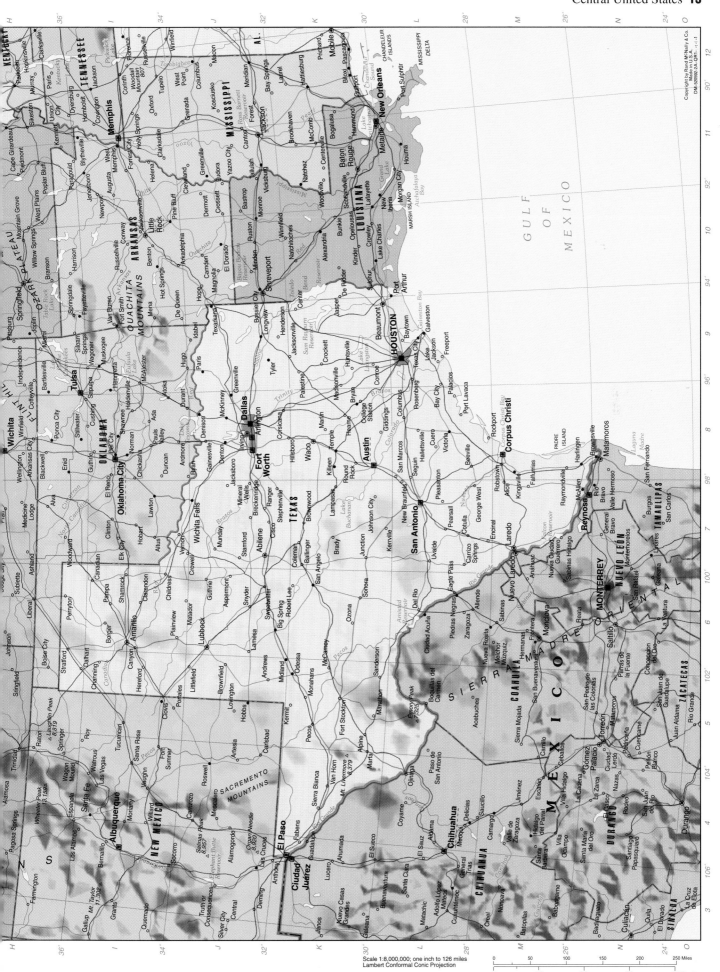

Scale 1:8,000,000; one inch to 126 miles
Lambert Conformal Conic Projection

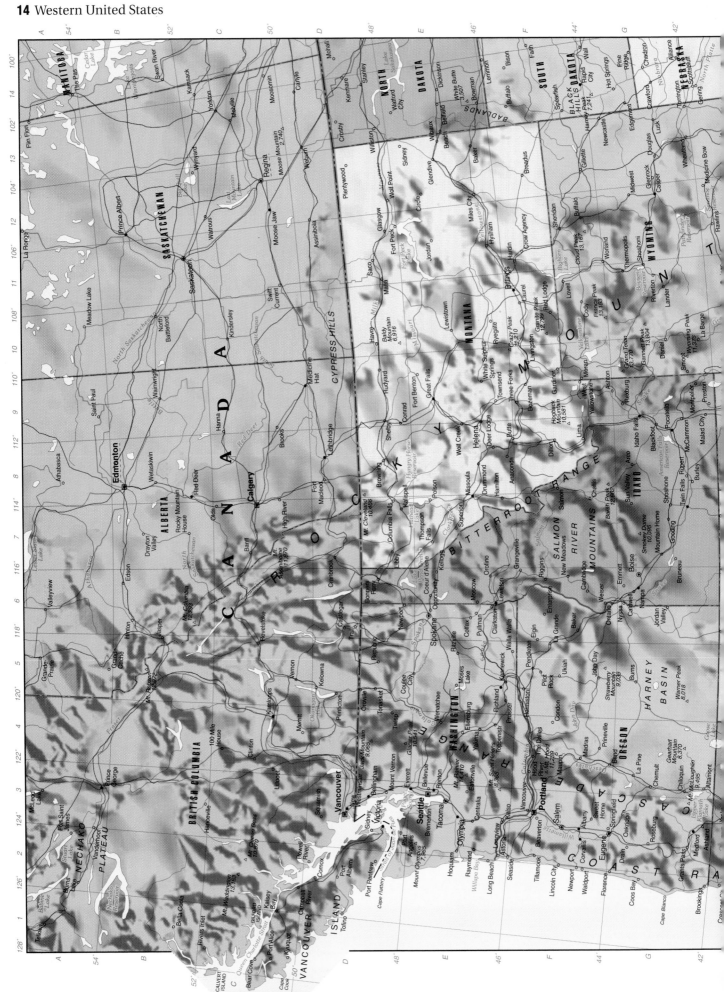

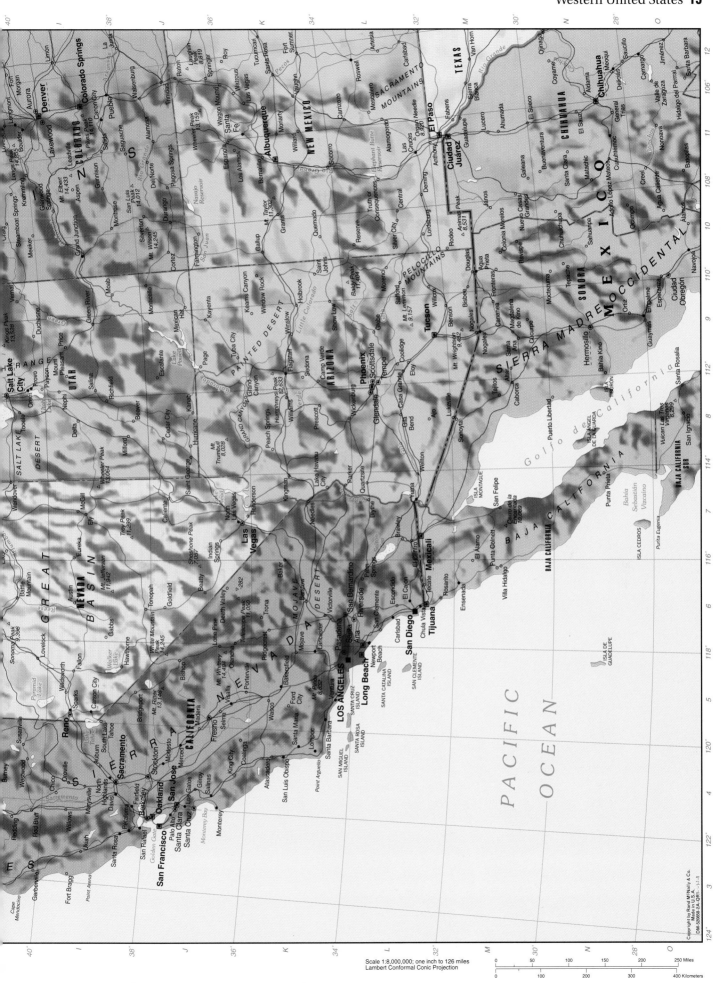

ATLANTIC OCEAN

CARIBBEAN SEA

Tropic of Cancer

WEST INDIES

GREATER ANTILLES

LESSER ANTILLES

WEST VIRGINIA
Lynchburg
Roanoke
Richmond
Petersburg
Norfolk
Portsmouth
Virginia Beach
VIRGINIA
Johnson City
Greensboro
Winston-Salem
Durham
Raleigh
Goldsboro
NORTH CAROLINA
Asheville
Spartanburg
Charlotte
Fayetteville
Cape Lookout
Columbia
Florence
Wilmington
SOUTH CAROLINA
Cape Fear
Augusta
Macon
Charleston
GEORGIA
Valdosta
Savannah
Jacksonville
Gainesville
Ocala
Daytona Beach
Orlando
Merritt Island
Cape Canaveral
Melbourne
Tampa
water
sburg
Lakeland
Fort Pierce
FLORIDA
Sarasota
Lake Okeechobee
West Palm Beach
Fort Myers
Freeport
Hialeah
Fort Lauderdale
Miami
Cape Sable
Nassau
BAHAMAS
Key West
NEW PROVIDENCE
ELEUTHERA
CAT ISLAND
FLORIDA KEYS
ANDROS
Straits of Florida
LONG ISLAND
ACKLINS
GREAT INAGUA
HAVANA
Matanzas
Cárdenas
Güines
Sagua la Grande
Placetas
Santa Clara
Cienfuegos
Morón
Ciego de Ávila
Nuevitas
Pinar del Río
Trinidad
Florida
CUBA
Camagüey
Holguín
Banes
Santa Cruz del Sur
ISLA DE LA JUVENTUD
Manzanillo
Bayamo
Palma Soriano
Guantánamo
Cabo Cruz
Santiago de Cuba
CAYMAN ISLANDS (U.K.)
George Town
Montego Bay
Spanish Town
Port Antonio
May Pen
Kingston
JAMAICA
TURKS AND CAICOS ISLANDS (U.K.)
CAICOS ISLANDS
Grand Turk
Monte Cristi
Cap-Haïtien
Puerto Plata
Santiago
San Francisco de Macorís
Gonaïves
Mao
La Vega
Saint-Marc
San Juan
Jérémie
Port-au-Prince
HAITI
HISPANIOLA
La Romana
SANTO DOMINGO
Barahona
DOMINICAN REPUBLIC
Cabo Rojo
San Juan
VIRGIN ISLANDS (U.S.)
BRITISH VIRGIN ISLANDS
Road Town
Mayagüez
Caguas
Charlotte Amalie
PUERTO RICO (U.S.)
Ponce
SAINT CROIX
ANGUILLA (U.K.)
The Valley
ANTIGUA AND BARBUDA
Basseterre
SAINT KITTS AND NEVIS
Saint John's
Plymouth
MONTSERRAT (U.K.)
Pointe-à-Pitre
GUADELOUPE (Fr.)
Basse-Terre
DOMINICA
Roseau
Fort-de-France
MARTINIQUE (Fr.)
SAINT LUCIA
Castries
Bridgetown
SAINT VINCENT AND THE GRENADINES
Kingstown
BARBADOS
GRENADA
Saint George's
TOBAGO
Port of Spain
TRINIDAD AND TOBAGO
TRINIDAD
San Fernando
Cabo de Gracias a Dios
Prinzapolka
ISLA DE SAN ANDRÉS (Col.)
Bluefields
NICARAGUA
ARUBA (Neth.)
Oranjestad
CURAÇAO
NETHERLANDS ANTILLES
BONAIRE
Willemstad
ISLA DE MARGARITA
Porlamar
Carúpano
Güiria
Punta Gallinas
Cabo de La Vela
Punta Fijo
Puerto Cumarebo
Cumaná
Morawhanna
Riohacha
Maicao
Coro
Marlborough
Santa Marta
Cristóbal Colón 19,029
Guarenas
Puerto La Cruz
Charity
Suddie
Georgetown
Barranquilla
Sabanalarga
Puerto Cabello
CARACAS
Barcelona
Parika
Bartica
MARACAIBO
Altagracia
Puerto
Cabello
Carora
Maracay
Valencia
Maturín
New Amsterdam
Soledad
Machiques
Cabimas
Guacara
Teques
Nieuw Nickerie
Cartagena
San Jacinto
Turbaco
Valledupar
Trujillo
Barquisimeto
Valle de la Pascua
Anaco
San José de Guanipa
Tucupita
San Onofre
Corozal
Lago de Maracaibo
Acarigua
El Tigre
GUYANA
Lorica
Cereté
Sincelejo
Valera
Guanare
Calabozo
Ciudad Guayana
Upata
Mount Roraima 9,432
Montería
Sahagún
El Banco
Mérida
Ocaña
Barinas
San Fernando
Ciudad Bolívar
Cerro Bolívar 2,631
San Marcos
Caucasia
Orinoco
Cerro Yaví 8,099
Auyán Tepuy
LA GRAN SABANA
PACARAIMA MTS.
Lethem
Turbo
Cúcuta
San Cristóbal
Guasdualito
Puerto
Ayacucho
Chigorodó
Pamplona
Bucaramanga
Floridablanca
Pico Bolívar 16,427
VENEZUELA
Cerro Mato 6,712
Barrancabermeja
ISLA DE COIBA
Yarumal
Riosucio
Puerto Berrío
Cerro Yaví
SURINAME
Cerro Marahuaca 8,461
Boa Vista
KANUKU MTS.
Bello
Itaguí
Duitama
Sogamoso
MEDELLÍN
La Dorada
Puerto
Ayacucho
Cacurí
KAMOA MTS.
Quibdó
Envigado
COLOMBIA
Cabo Corrientes
Manizales
Honda
Pereira
Nevado del Ruiz 17,717
BRAZIL
Cartago
Armenia
ACARAI MTS.
Punta Magdalena
Ibagué
BOGOTÁ
Buga
Tuluá
Villavicencio
Espinal
Buenaventura
CALI
Palmira
San Martín
Neiva
San Carlos de Río Negro
Vichada
Guaviare
Meta
Tomo
Magdalena
PANAMA
Golfo de los Mosquitos
Colón
Panama
San José
Puerto Limón
Volcán Chirripó 12,530
David
San Isidro
Golfo de San Blas
La Chorrera
Aguadulce
Chitré
Golfo de Panamá
Punta Mala
ISTMO DE PANAMA
Golfo del Darién
SERRANIA DE PERIJA
Puerto Mariato
Punta Marzo

PACIFIC OCEAN

Golfo de California

BAJA CALIFORNIA

BAJA CALIFORNIA SUR

SONORA

CHIHUAHUA

SIERRA MADRE OCCIDENTAL

DURANGO

SINALOA

ZACATECAS

NAYARIT

JALISCO

COLIMA

ARIZONA

NEW MEXICO

Tijuana

Mexicali

El Paso

Ciudad Juárez

Chihuahua

Hermosillo

Ciudad Obregón

Guaymas

Culiacán

Mazatlán

Durango

Tepic

GUADALAJARA

Tropic of Cancer

Isla Guadalupe

Islas Revillagigedo (Mex.)

Isla Clarión (Mex.)

Isla Socorro

Isla San Benedicto

Islas Marías

GULF OF MEXICO

Bahía de Campeche

TEXAS

LOUISIANA

MISSISSIPPI

ALABAMA

FLORIDA

UNITED STATES

TAMAULIPAS

NUEVO LEÓN

SAN LUIS POTOSÍ

HIDALGO

VERACRUZ

TABASCO

CAMPECHE

YUCATÁN

QUINTANA ROO

YUCATÁN PENINSULA

GUATEMALA

BELIZE

CHIAPAS

OAXACA

GUERRERO

MORELOS

PUEBLA

TLAXCALA

Scale 1:8,000,000; one inch to 126 miles
Lambert Conformal Conic Projection

Tropic of Cancer

U.S.

GULF OF MEXICO

Miami

Cape Sable

BAHAMAS

Tropic of Cancer

A

HAVANA

CUBA

Mérida

YUCATAN PENINSULA

Canal de Yucatán

MEXICO

GUATEMALA

BELIZE
Belmopan

Gulf of Honduras

HONDURAS

Tegucigalpa

San Salvador

EL SALVADOR

NICARAGUA

Managua

Lago de Nicaragua

San José

COSTA RICA

Panamá

PANAMA

Golfo de Panamá

JAMAICA

Kingston

Port-au-Prince

HAITI

DOMINICAN REPUBLIC

SANTO DOMINGO

PUERTO RICO (U.S.)

GUADELOUPE (Fr.)

SAINT LUCIA

CARIBBEAN SEA

LESSER ANTILLES

ATLANTIC OCEAN

B

Barranquilla

Cartagena

Punta Gallinas

MARACAIBO

CARACAS

Barquisimeto

TRINIDAD AND TOBAGO

Boca Grande

Cúcuta

Palmarito

LLANOS

Orinoco

Georgetown

Paramaribo

Cayenne

Cabo Caciporé

Cabo Norte

C

Bucaramanga

VENEZUELA

GUYANA

SURINAME

FRENCH GUIANA

MEDELLÍN

Nev. del Tolima 17,110

BOGOTÁ

CALI

COLOMBIA

Cacurí

PAKARAIMA MTS.

Boa Vista

Punta Magdalena

Nev. del Huila 18,865

San Carlos de Río Negro

Macapá

Ilha de Marajó

Baía de Marajó

Punta Galera

QUITO

Cayambe 18,996

Lérida

Taraquá

MANAUS

Santarém

Belém

São Luis

Equator

GALÁPAGOS ISLANDS (Ec.)

ECUADOR

GUAYAQUIL

Iquitos

Tamaniquá

ILHA FERNANDO DE NORONHA

Equator

Punta Pariñas

Eirunepé

Juruá

B R A Z I L

Conceição

Imperatriz

Fortaleza

Teresina

Natal

D

Chiclayo

Porto Velho

Ji-Paraná

Alta Floresta

Conceição do Araguaia

Cabo de São Roque

RECIFE

Nev. Huascarán 22,133

PLANALTO DO MATO GROSSO

Represa de Sobradinho

Feira de Santana

Aracaju

Callao

Cusco

Puerto Heath

Nev. Illampu 21,066

Trinidad

Cuiabá

SALVADOR

Lima

Punta Carreta

Lago Titicaca

LA PAZ

Golânia

BRASÍLIA

Itabuna

E

Arequipa

Oruro

Nev. Sajama 21,483

BOLIVIA

Santa Cruz de la Sierra

Sucre

Uberlândia

Represa de Três Marias

Ponta da Baleia

Iquique

BELO HORIZONTE

Cabo de São Tomé

Antofagasta

GRAN CHACO

PARAGUAY

Anambaí

Londrina

SÃO PAULO

RIO DE JANEIRO

Tropic of Capricorn

PACIFIC OCEAN

ISLA SAN AMBROSIO (Chile)

Punta Ballenita

Nev. Ojos del Salado 22,615

Asunción

Santo André

Tropic of Capricorn

ISLA SAN FÉLIX (Chile)

Punta Cachos

San Miguel de Tucumán

Santiago del Estero

Santa Maria

Florianópolis

F

ARCHIPIÉLAGO JUAN FERNÁNDEZ (Chile)

Valparaíso

Santiago

CÓRDOBA

Cerro Aconcagua 22,831

ROSARIO

Goya

Santa Fe

URUGUAY

Ponta do Bojuru

PORTO ALEGRE

Lagoa dos Patos

Lagoa Mirim

BUENOS AIRES

MONTEVIDEO

Concepción

Punta Morguilla

La Plata

Punta del Este

Río de la Plata

9

Valdivia

Bahía Blanca

Neuquén

Mar del Plata

G

Cabo Quedal

Golfo San Matías

Península Valdés

ISLA GRANDE DE CHILOÉ

A R G E N T I N A

ATLANTIC OCEAN

ARCHIPIÉLAGO DE LOS CHONOS

Cabo dos Bahías

Golfo San Jorge

Comodoro Rivadavia

TRISTAN DA CUNHA GROUP (St. Helena)

Península de Taitao

Punta Medanoso

GOUGH ISLAND (St. Helena)

ISLA WELLINGTON

PATAGONIA

Bahía Grande

FALKLAND ISLANDS (U.K.)

H

Cabo Deseado

Punta Arenas

Strait of Magellan

WEST FALKLAND

Stanley

EAST FALKLAND

ISLA SANTA INÉS

TIERRA DEL FUEGO

Cape Horn (Cabo de Hornos)

SOUTH GEORGIA (U.K.)

Drake Passage

SOUTH SANDWICH ISLANDS (U.K.)

BOUVET (Nor.)

I

SOUTH SHETLAND ISLANDS (U.K.)

SOUTH ORKNEY ISLANDS (U.K.)

Antarctic Circle

ALEXANDER ISLAND

Antarctic Peninsula

0 200 400 600 800 1000 Miles

0 300 600 900 1200 1500 Kilometers

Scale 1:45,000,000; one inch to 710 miles
Lambert Azimuthal, Equal Area Projection

Scale 1:16,000,000; one inch to 252 miles
Lambert Conformal Conic Projection

| 0 | 100 | 200 | 300 | 400 | 500 Miles |

| 0 | 200 | 400 | 600 | 800 Kilometers |

NICARAGUA

COSTA RICA

Lago de Nicaragua
ISLA DE OMETEPE
Cabo Santa Elena
Puntarenas
Alajuela
Puerto Limón
San José
San Isidro
Volcán Irazú 11,260
Cerro Chirripó 12,530
Volcán Barú 11,401
David
Puerto Armuelles
Punta Burica
Golfo de Chiriquí
Santiago
Aguadulce
Chitré
ISLA DE COIBA
Punta Mariato
Peninsula de Azuero
Punta Mala
PANAMÁ
Panamá
La Chorrera
Golfo de Panamá
ISLA DEL REY
ISTMO
Colón
Golfo de los Mosquitos

ARUBA (Neth.)
NETHERLANDS ANTILLES
CURAÇAO BONAIRE
Oranjestad
Willemstad
Punta Gallinas
Cabo de La Vela
Peninsula de la Guajira
Peninsula de Paraguaná
Punto Fijo
Golfo de Venezuela
Coro
Puerto Cumarebo
ISLA DE MARGARITA
Porlamar
Cumaná
Barcelona
Punta Fijo

Santa Marta
Riohacha
Maicao
CARACAS
Petare
Guarenas
Guacara
Puerto La Cruz
Anaco
San José de Guanipa

Barranquilla
Soledad
Sabanalarga
Ciénaga
Pico Cristóbal Colón 19,029
MARACAIBO
Altagracia
Cabimas
Carora
Barquisimeto
VALENCIA
Maracay

Cartagena
Plato
Valledupar
Machiques
Lago de Maracaibo
Trujillo
Valera
Acarigua
Guanare
El Tigre

San Jacinto
Tucaco
San Onofre
Sincelejo
Corozal
El Banco
Ocaña
Mérida
Pico Bolívar 16,427
Barinas
Valle de la Pascua

Lorica
Cereté
Sahagún
CÚCUTA
San Cristóbal
San Fernando
Calabozo

Montería
San Marcos
Caucasia
Pamplona
BUCARAMANGA
Floridablanca
Guasdualito
Apure
Arauca

Turbo
Chigorodó
Barrancabermeja
Puerto Berrío
Yarumal
Bello
Itagüí
MEDELLÍN
Envigado
Quibdó
Cabo Corrientes
La Dorada
Honda
Sogamoso
Duitama
Tunja
Yopal
Meta

VENEZUELA
Cerro Mato 6,112
Puerto Ayacucho
Ciudad Guayana
Cerro Bolívar 2,631
Embalse de Guri
Ciudad Bolívar
Orinoco
Palmarito
Tomo
Cerro Yaví 8,009
Cacurí
Anauá

Manizales
Pereira
Cartago
Armenia
CALI
Palmira
Tuluá
Buga
Nev. del Tolima 17,110
Nev. del Huila 18,865
BOGOTÁ
Ibagué
Espinal
Villavicencio
San Martín
Neiva
San José del Guaviare
Vichada
Guaviare
COLOMBIA
Cerro Marahuaca 9,461
SIERRA PARIMA
SIERRA DE CURUPIRA

Buenaventura
Punta Magdalena
Popayán
Pitalito
Pasto
Florencia
Serranía de la Macarena
Inírida
Guainía
San Carlos de Río Negro
Pico da Neblina 9,888
Negro

Tumaco
Cabo Manglares
Ipiales
Tulcán
Ibarra
Cayambe 18,996
Putumayo
Caquetá
Apaporis
Vaupés
Lérida
Taraqua

Esmeraldas
Punta Galera
QUITO
ECUADOR
Cabo Pasado
Chone
Cotopaxi 19,347
Ambato
Chimborazo 20,702
Riobamba
Napo
Amazonas
Iquitos
Leticia
AMAZONAS
Tefé
Juruá
Juruá

Manta
Portoviejo
Jipijapa
Vinces
Babahoyo
Milagro
Vol. Sangay 17,159
Cabo San Lorenzo
Punta Santa Elena
GUAYAQUIL
Cañar
Cuenca
Golfo de Guayaquil
ISLA PUNA
Machala
Pasaje
Loja
Tumbes

SAN CRISTÓBAL
GALAPAGOS ISLANDS
(ARCHIPIELAGO DE COLÓN)
(Ecuador)
Equator
ISLA DE MALPELO (Colombia)
ISLA DEL COCO (Costa Rica)

CORDILLERA OCCIDENTAL
CORDILLERA ORIENTAL
CORDILLERA DEL CÓNDOR

Talara
Punta Pariñas
Sullana
Piura
Castilla
Sechura
Jaén
Marañón
Moyobamba
Chachapoyas
Yurimaguas
Ucayali
Eirunepé
Lábrea
Purus

Lambayeque
Chiclayo
Cajamarca
Chocope
Pacasmayo
Trujillo
Cruzeiro do Sul
ACRE
Rio Branco
Porto Velho
Ariquemes
RONDÔNIA

Chimbote
Nev. Huascarán 22,133
Tingo Maria
Huánuco
Pucallpa
Huaraz
CORDILLERA ORIENTAL
Huarmey
Nevado Yerupaja 21,765
Cerro de Pasco
PERU
Guajará-Mirim

Pativilca
Huacho
Punta Lachay
Huaral
Huaura
La Oroya
Tarma
Chosica
Callao
LIMA
Vitarte
Mala
Huancayo
Huancavelica
Río de los Pedros
Puerto Maldonado
Puerto Heath

Chincha Alta
Bahía de Paracas
Pisco
Ica
Punta Carreta
Ayacucho
Abancay
Machupicchu
Cusco
Nevado Ausangate 20,945
Ayaviri
Benj
Madre de Dios
Puerto
Maldonado
Trinidad

Nazca
Punta Parada
CORDILLERA DE HUANZO
Nevado Coropuna 20,686
Juliaca
Lago Titicaca
Nev. Illampu 21,066
BOLIVIA
San Miguel

Nevado Chachani 19,931
Puno
Arequipa
Volcán Misti 19,101
Nev. Illimani 20,741
LA PAZ
Cochabamba

Camaná
Mollendo
Moquegua
Volcán Tutupaca 19,898
CORDILLERA OCCIDENTAL
Oruro
Santa Cruz de la Sierra
Lago Poopó

PACIFIC OCEAN

Ilo
Tacna
Arica
Nev. Sajama 21,463
ANDES
ALTIPLANO
Sucre

Pisagua
Iquique
Pozo Almonte
Potosí

Tocopilla
Chuquicamata
Calama
Cerro Licancabur 19,409
Tarija
CHILE
ARGENTINA
Vilama

0 100 200 300 400 500 Miles
0 200 400 600 800 Kilometers

ATLANTIC OCEAN

TOBAGO
TRINIDAD AND TOBAGO
Port of Spain
TRINIDAD
San Fernando

Morawhanna
Marlborough
Charity Suddie
Parika Georgetown
Bartica Enmore
New Amsterdam
Nieuw
Nickerie Nieuw Amsterdam
Groningen Paramaribo
Albina Iracoubo
GUYANA Kwakoegron Saint-Laurent- Sinnamary
du-Maroni Kourou
Mount Roraima 9,432 Brokopondo Cayenne
Stuwmeer Saint-Élie
PAKARAIMA MTS. Guisanbourg
SURINAME Quanary
a Vista Lethem FRENCH
KANUKU Juliana Top 4,035 GUIANA Cabo Cacipore
MTS. Saül
KAMOA ACARAI MTS.
MTS. TUMUC-HUMAC MOUNTAINS AMAPÁ

ILHA DE MARACÁ
Cabo Norte
ILHA BAILIQUE
ILHA DO CURUÁ
ILHA JANAUCU
Macapá ILHA CAVIANA DE FORA
ILHA MEXIANA
ILHA Cabo Maguari
GRANDE ILHA DE Souré Baía de Marajó
DO GURUPÁ MARAJÓ Belém Capanema Bragança
Oriximiná Breves Abaetetuba Castanhal Carutapera
Faro Portel Cametá São
MANAUS Santarém Luis Parnaíba Camocim
Manacapuru Macoatiara Itapipoca
Maués Altamira Pindaré Mirim Coroatá Sobral Fortaleza
Tucuruí Bacabal Codó Piripiri Campo Maracanaú
Itaituba Represa de Pedreiras Maior Pacajus
Tucuruí Caxias CEARÁ Quixadá Mossoró
Novo Maraba Timon Teresina Crateus Cabo de São Roque
Aripuanã PARÁ SERRA DOS CARAJÁS Imperatriz MARANHÃO Jaguaribe RIO GRANDE DO NORTE Natal
S Nazaré São João dos Igautu Caicó
Conceicao Araguaína Tocantinópolis Patos Juazeiro Patos Guarabira
Carolina Floriano do Norte PARAÍBA João
Balsas Picos Crato Campina Pessoa
Alta Floresta Conceição Oeiras PIAUÍ Salgueiro Grande Timbaúba
SERRA DOS APIACAS da Araguaia Curupa PERNAMBUCO Olinda
SERRA Represa Boa Arcoverde Caruaru RECIFE
DO ESPINHO Esperança Garanhuns Palmeira dos
BRAZIL Palmas Petrolina Paulo Afonso Indios Palmares
MATO GROSSO Porto Nacional Juazeiro ALAGOAS
Maceió
SERRA DO NORTE Senhor do Arapiraca
Alta Floresta Bonfim Penedo
Vilhena SERRA DO TOMBADOR TOCANTINS Irecê SERGIPE
Gurupi Jacobina Aracaju
SERRA DO RONCADOR Barreiras Ibotirama Feira de
SERRA FORMOSA Santana Esplanada
Diamantino Porangatu Santana BAHIA Alagoinhas
MATO GROSSO SERRA Bom Jesus Itaberaba Camaçari
PLANALTO DOURADA da Lapa Valença SALVADOR
SERRA DOS PARECIS DO MATO Guanambi Jequié
GROSSO Brumado Ipiaú Ilhéus
Cuiabá Formosa Januária Vitória da Itabuna Itapetinga
Cáceres BRASÍLIA São Conquista Canavieiras
Jaciara DISTRITO FEDERAL Francisco Pedra Azul Belmonte
Barra do Garças Luziânia Unaí Salinas Almenara
Rondonópolis Inhumas Montes Claros Itaobim
Juçara Ipora Anápolis Paracatu Itamaraju
Caiapônia Goiânia Bocaiuva Teófilo Otoni Ponta da Baleia
Coxim GOIÁS Pires do João Pirapora Nanuque
Rio Verde de Mineiros Jataí Rio Pinheiro Nanuque
Mato Grosso Pontalina Patos de MINAS São Mateus
Harumá Ilumbiara Minas GERAIS Governador
Corumbá Araguari Curvelo Valadares Linhares
MATO GROSSO Ituiutaba Campina Sete Lagoas Araxá Ipatinga Colatina
DO SUL Uberlândia Verde Vitória
Puerto Bahía Miranda Camapuã Paranaíba Frutal BELO Vila Velha
Negra Aquidauana Uberaba HORIZONTE Ponte Nova Itaguaí
Campo Grande Três Lagoas Franca São João Cachoeiro de Itapemirim
São José do del Rei
Três Lagoas Rio Preto Lavras Juiz de Fora Cabo de São Tomé
Aracatuba Araraquara Poços de Caldas RIO DE Campos
SÃO PAULO São Carlos Volta JANEIRO Nova Friburgo
Douradas Tupã Lins Redonda Três Rios
Pedro Juan Ponta Porã Marília Piracicaba Taubaté Nova Iguaçu Niterói
Caballero Assis Campinas São José dos Campos RIO DE JANEIRO
PARAGUAY Bauru Campinas
São José dos Campos
Sorocaba SÃO PAULO
Santo André Santos
São Vicente Tropic of Capricorn

Equator

Cabo de São Roque

Represa de
Sobradinho

São Francisco

Represa de
Tres Marias

SERRA DO ESPINHAÇO

SERRA DO MAR

Copyright by Rand McNally & Co.
Made in U.S.A.
DM-549100-2A-QR1- - 1-1-1

Scale 1:16,000,000; one inch to 252 miles
Lambert Azimuthal, Equal Area Projection

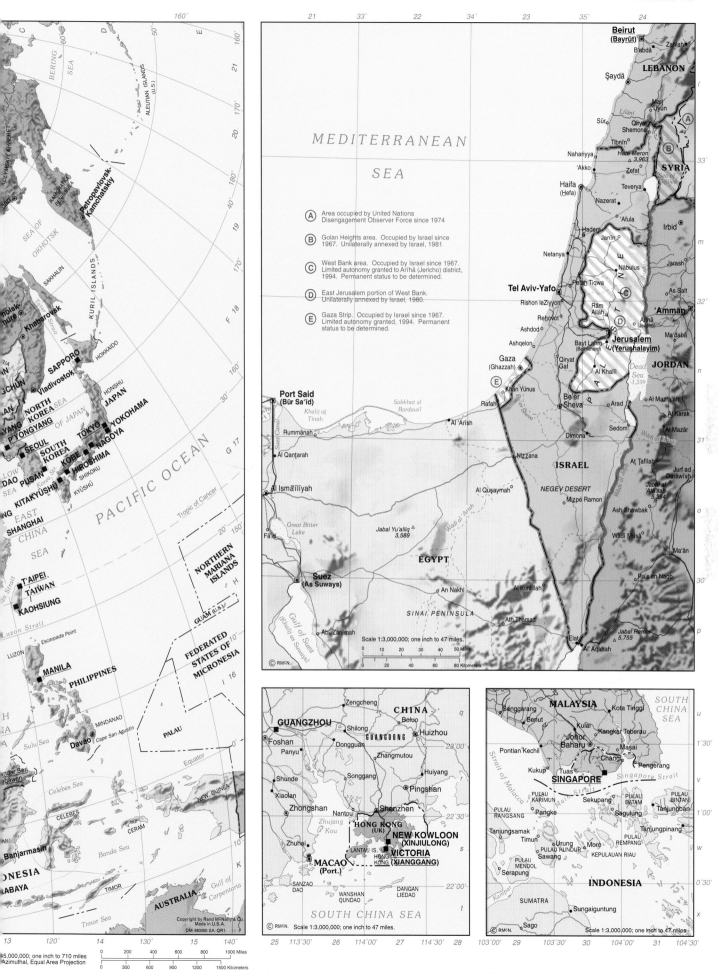

ATLANTIC

OCEAN

ICELAND
Reykjavik
Akureyri
Djúpivogur
Stokksnes
Hekla 4.892
Horn

NORWEGIAN
SEA

Arctic Circle

LOFOTEN VESTERÅLEN
Narvik
Kebnekaise 6.926

FAEROE IS.
(Den.)
Tórshavn

NORWAY
SWEDEN
Trondheim
Umeå
Östersund
Örnsköldsvik
Härnösand
Galdhøpiggen 8.100
Dombås
Lillehammer
Särna
Gävle
Sognafjorden
Bergen
Oslo
Stavanger
Lindesnes
Uppsala
Stockholm
Norrköping
Linköping
GOTLAND
Visby
ÖLAND
Kolkas Rags
Liepāja

SHETLAND
ISLANDS
Lerwick

HEBRIDES
Wick
Duncansby Head
ORKNEY
ISLANDS
SCOTLAND
GRAMPIAN MTS
Aberdeen
Kinnaird Head
Glasgow
Dundee
Edinburgh
CHEVIOT HILLS
Newcastle upon Tyne

NORTH
SEA

Skagerrak
Grenen
Ålborg
DENM.
Kattegat
Copenhagen
(København)
Malmö
Göteborg
Vänern
Vättern
Turku

BALTIC SEA

Klaipėda
Kalin
RUS
BORNHOLM
(Den.)

IRELAND
Bloody Foreland
Achill Head
Galway
Loop Head
Limerick
Mizen Head
Cork

NORTHERN IRELAND
Belfast
Dublin
Liverpool
Irish Sea

UNITED
KINGDOM
Kingston upon Hull
Manchester
Leicester
BIRMINGHAM
WALES
ENGLAND
Cardiff
Southampton
The Hague ('s-Gravenhage)
LONDON
Portsmouth
Plymouth
Lizard Point
English Channel
Land's End
Hartland Point
St. George's Channel

NETHERLANDS
Amsterdam
Rotterdam
Bremerhaven
Kiel
Rostock
HAMBURG
Bremen
Hannover
Magdeburg
BERLIN
Szczecin
Gdańsk
Toruń
POLAN
Poznań
Łódź
WAR
(WARS
L
Wrocław
Katowice
Krak

BELGIUM
Brussels
Essen
Bonn
Dresden
Leipzig
GERMANY
Frankfurt
Mainz
LUX.
Luxembourg
Lille
Le Havre
Rouen
Reims
Cherbourg
CHANNEL IS. (U.K.)
Brest
Pointe du Raz
Rennes
PARIS
Orléans
Tours
Nantes

FRANCE
Pointe de la Coubre
Bay of Biscay
Pointe de la Coubre
Limoges
Dijon
Strasbourg
Mulhouse
Nürnberg
Stuttgart
MUNICH
(MÜNCHEN)
PRAGUE
(PRAHA)
SUDETES
Plzeň
CZECH
REPUBLIC
Ostrava
SLOVAKIA
Bratislava
VIENNA
(WIEN)
Győr
Debrece
BUDAPEST
HUNGARY
Szeged
Timi
AUSTRIA
Graz
Großglockner 3.457
LIECH.
SWITZERLAND
Zürich
Bern
Lausanne
Genève
Mont Blanc 4.807
Lyon
Grenoble
SLO.
Ljubljana
Zagreb
CROATIA
BELGRADE
(BEOGRAD)
BOSNIA AND
HERZEGOVINA
Sarajevo
YUGOSLA
Venice (Venezia)
Turin (Torino)
MILAN
(MILANO)
Genoa
(Genova)
Bologna
La Spezia
Ligurian Sea
SAN
MARINO
Florence
(Firenze)
Ancona
Split
Toulouse
ANDORRA
PYRENEES
Nîmes
Avign
Marseille
Golfe du Lion
MONACO
Toulon
Livorno
ITALY
ADRIATIC SEA
ALBANIA
Tirane
Bari
Cap Corse
CORSICA
(Fr.)
Ajaccio
ROME
(ROMA)
NAPLES
(NAPOLI)
Vesuvius 1.190
Taranto
Lecce
Cap de Creus
Cap de la Nau

La Coruña
Cabo Ortegal
Cabo de Finisterre
Gijón
Oviedo
Santander
Vigo
Cabo Mondego
Porto
Bilbao
Donostia
Logroño
Zaragoza
Ebro
PORTUGAL
Coimbra
SPAIN
Valladolid
Salamanca
Cabo da Roca
Lisbon
(Lisboa)
Badajoz
Toledo
MADRID
SIERRA MORENA
Córdoba
Albacete
Cabo de São Vicente
Faro
Sevilla
Granada
Murcia
Cádiz
SISTEMAS BÉTICOS
Strait of Gibraltar
Málaga
Almería
Cartagena
Tanger
Ceuta (Sp.)
GIBRALTAR (U.K.)
Tétouan
Melilla (Sp.)
Wahran
València
BALEARIC ISLANDS
Palma
MALLORCA
MENORCA
EIVISSA
Cabo de Palos
Alacant
BARCELONA
Tarragona

Sassari
SARDINIA
(It.)
Cagliari
Capo Comino
Capo Spartivento
TYRRHENIAN
SEA
Capo Palinuro
Cosenza
Capo Colonna
Catanzaro
Palermo
Messina
Mt. Etna 10.902
Catania
IONIAN
SEA
Capo Passero
I. DI
PANTELLERIA
(It.)
SICILY
Cap Bon
Valletta
MALTA
MEDITERRANEAN

ALGIERS
(EL DJAZAÏR)
Annaba
Tunis
TUNISIA
Rabat
MOROCCO
Meknès
Fès
CASABLANCA
ATLAS MOUNTAINS
Qacentina
Batna
ALGERIA
El Djelfa
Laghouat
Sousse
Beni-Mellal
Marrakech
Cap Rhir

Scale 1:16,000,000; one inch to 252 miles
Lambert Conformal Conic Projection

ARCTIC OCEAN

LOFOTEN VESTERÅLEN

Na

Bodø

NORWEGIAN

SEA

Mo

Mosjøen

Serse

Storm

Namsos

Steinkjer

Vilhelmine

Åse

ICELAND

Horn
Siglufjör-ur
GRIMSEY
Húsavík
Akureyri
Rifstangi
Fontur
akur

Snæfellsnes
Breiðafjörður
Stykkishólmur
Faxaflói
Reykjavík
Reykjanes
Keflavík
Thingvellir
Selfoss
Hekla
4.892
Hvannadalshnúkur
6.952
Djúpivogur
Stokksnes
Vestmannaeyjar

ARCTIC OCEAN

Arctic Circle

Trondheim

Levanger
Strömsund

SWEDEN

Ålesund
Dombås
Ostersund
Sollefte

Galdhøpiggen
8,100
Särna
Hätr

NORWAY

Sognafjorden
Ljungan

FAEROE
ISLANDS
(Den.)
Tórshavn

Lågen

Lillehammer
Bollnäs

Bergen
Hamar
Mora
Falun
Sandvi

Borlänge

OSLO
Drammen
Lillestrøm

Uppsa

ATLANTIC

ROCKALL
(U.K.)

Haugesund
Arvika
Karlstad
Västerås
Stock

Stavanger
Skien
Porsgrunn
Sandefjord
Halden
Säffle
Örebro
Eskilstuna

OCEAN

SHETLAND
ISLANDS

RONA

Lerwick
Sumburgh Head

Egersund
Arendal

Vänern
Karlskoga
Motala
Norr
Linköping

Lindesnes
Mandal
Kristiansand
Uddevalla
Skövde
Vetlanda
Väst

SAINT
KILDA

ORKNEY
ISLANDS

Stornoway
Cape Wrath
Kirkwall
Duncansby Head
Wick

Skagerrak
Fredriks-
havn
Grenen
Göteborg
Jönköping
Borås
Varberg
Värnamo
Ljungby
Oskarshamn

HEBRIDES
The Minch

Tobermory
Inverness
Moray Firth
Kinnaird Head

Viborg
Ålborg
Kattegat
Randers
Fornæs
Halmstad
Kalmar
Borg
ÖLAN

Ben Nevis
4.406
GRAMPIAN MTS.
SCOTLAND
Perth
Dundee
Aberdeen

Holstebro
DENMARK
Århus
Helsingborg
Karlshamn
Karlskrona

BRITISH
ISLES

Stirling
Firth of Forth

NORTH

Esbjerg
Kolding
Odense
SJÆLLAND
Copenhagen
(København)
Malmö
Trelleborg

BORNHOLM
(Den.)

BAL

Glasgow
Edinburgh
UNITED
GREAT

Londonderry
NORTHERN
IRELAND
Ballymena
Belfast
Bangor
Ayr
Kilmarnock
Dumfries
Stranraer
CHEVIOT
HILLS
Newcastle
upon Tyne
Sunderland

SEA

Flensburg
Schleswig
LOLLAND
Nykøbing
Kap Arkona
Stralsund

Rønne

North Channel

Kiel

Bloody Foreland
Malin Head
Donegal Bay
Erris Head
Achill Head
Sligo
Dundalk
ISLE OF MAN
(U.K.)
Douglas
Whitehaven
Carlisle
Middlesbrough

Cuxhaven
Wilhelmshaven
Itzehoe
Lübeck
Neubrandenburg
Rostock
Schwerin
Wismar
Kołobrzeg
Świnoujście
Szczecinek
Koszali

Clifden
IRELAND
Galway

Irish
Sea

Liverpool
ENGLAND
Bradford
York
Scarborough

Leeuwarden
Groningen
HAMBURG
Wittenberge
Stargard
Szczecin

Loop Head

Dublin

Stoke on Trent
Chester
Manchester
Sheffield
Grimsby

Den Helder
NETHERLANDS
Oldenburg
Bremerhaven
Bremen
BERLIN
Gorzów Wielkopols
Bydg

Limerick
Tipperary
Carlow
KINGDOM

Kingston upon Hull

Leeuwarden
Osnabrück
Hannover
Braunschweig
Magdeburg
Potsdam
Fürstenwalde

Poznań

Carrauntoohil
3.406
Clonmel

Shrewsbury
Derby
Nottingham
Norwich

BRITAIN

Haarlem
Amsterdam
Leiden
Utrecht
Münster
Bielefeld
Hildesheim
Dessau
Halle
Cottbus
Zielona Góra
Głogów

Cork
Kinsale
Mizen
Head
Bantry

St. George's Channel

BIRMINGHAM
WALES
Coventry
Leicester

GERMANY

NETHERLANDS

Leipzig
Zary
Legnica

Milford
Haven
Hereford
Northampton
Cambridge
Great
Yarmouth

Den Haag
Rotterdam
Hannover
Göttingen
Riesa

Waterford
Dungarvan

CELTIC SEA

Cardiff
Newport
Bristol
Oxford
LONDON

The Hague
('s-Gravenhage)
Essen
Dortmund
Kassel
Erfurt
Chemnitz
Dresden
Wałbrzych
W

ISLES OF SCILLY

Swansea

Brugge
Antwerpen
Wuppertal
Siegen
Kassel
Coburg

Exeter
Southampton
Reading
Brighton
Dover

Gent
BELGIUM
Düsseldorf
Köln
Bonn
Koblenz
Suhl
Zwickau
Mladá
Chomutov
Kladno
PRAGUE
(PRAHA)
Hradec
Kralove

Penzance
Plymouth
Bournemouth
Portsmouth
Start Point

Calais
Strait of Dover
Brussels
(Bruxelles)
Liège
Maastricht
Namur
Charleroi
LUX.
Trier
Wiesbaden
Frankfurt
Offenbach
Mainz
Würzburg
Cheb
CZECH REPUBLIC
Os

Land's End
Lizard Point

English Channel
Cap de la Hague
Cherbourg

GUERNSEY
(U.K.)
Saint Austell
Hartland Point
Pointe de Saint-Mathieu

CHANNEL IS.
JERSEY (U.K.)

Dieppe
Lille
Mons
Namur
Luxembourg
Mannheim
Heilbronn
Heidelberg
Nürnberg
Plzeň

Abbeville
Lens
Amiens
Saint-
Quentin
Laon
Mézières
Reims
Koblenz
Saarbrücken
Karlsruhe

Pointe du Raz
Brest
Quimper

Cap de la Hague
Golfe de
Saint Malo
Le Havre
Rouen
Compiègne
Oise

SUDE

Lorient

FRANCE

Caen
Évreux
PARIS
Châlons-
sur-Marne
Metz

Vannes
Rennes
Saint-Brieuc
Saint-Malo
Alençon
Chartres
Seine
Le Mans
Châteaux
Saint-Dizier

Olomouc

Laval

Scale 1:10,000,000; one inch to 158 miles
Lambert Conformal Conic Projection

| 0 | 50 | 100 | 150 | 200 | 250 | 300 Miles |

| 0 | 100 | 200 | 300 | 400 | 500 Kilometers |

ATLANTIC OCEAN

CELTIC SEA

NORTH SEA

Bay of Biscay

English Channel

Irish Sea

St. George's Channel

LIGURIAN SEA

TYRRHE... SEA

MEDITE...

IRELAND
NORTHERN IRELAND
SCOTLAND
UNITED KINGDOM
ENGLAND
WALES
GREAT BRITAIN
DENMARK
NETHERLANDS
BELGIUM
GERMANY
LUX.
FRANCE
SWITZERLAND
LIECHTENSTEIN
ANDORRA
SPAIN
PORTUGAL
MONACO
MOROCCO
ALGERIA
TUNISIA
VATICAN C...
SARDINIA (It.)
CORSICA (Fr.)
BALEARIC ISLANDS (Sp.)
BRITISH ISLES

Bloody Foreland, Malin Head, Glasgow, Edinburgh, Londonderry, Belfast, Bangor, Newcastle upon Tyne, Sunderland, Middlesbrough, Scarborough, York, Kingston upon Hull, Grimsby, Sheffield, Nottingham, Leicester, Norwich, Cambridge, Great Yarmouth, Ipswich, LONDON, Dover, Brighton, Portsmouth, Southampton, Bournemouth, Exeter, Plymouth, Penzance, Cardiff, Bristol, Reading, Oxford, Swansea, Newport, Hereford, BIRMINGHAM, Coventry, Northampton, Derby, Stoke on Trent, Chester, Shrewsbury, Liverpool, Manchester, Bradford, Blackpool, Preston, Whitehaven, Carlisle, Stranraer, Dumfries, Kilmarnock, Ayr, Douglas, ISLE OF MAN (U.K.)

Dublin, Galway, Sligo, Dundalk, Limerick, Cork, Waterford, Wexford, Clonmel, Tipperary, Kilkee, Loop Head, Carrauntochill 3,406, Bantry, Mizen Head, Kinsale, Dungarvan, Carlow, Athlone, Clifden, Achill Head, Erris Head, Kilmarnock

GUERNSEY (U.K.), JERSEY (U.K.), CHANNEL IS., Golfe de Saint-Malo

Cap de la Hague, Cherbourg, Le Havre, Dieppe, Abbeville, Calais, Lille, Lens, Amiens, Saint-Quentin, Mézières, Laon, Reims, Metz, Nancy, Strasbourg, Épinal, Mulhouse, Saint-Brieuc, Saint-Malo, Rennes, Caen, Évreux, Rouen, Compiègne, Oise, Marne, PARIS, Troyes, Chaumont, Saint-Dizier, Châlons-sur-Marne, Brest, Quimper, Pointe du Raz, Pointe de Saint-Mathieu, Lorient, Vannes, Laval, Le Mans, Angers, Alençon, Chartres, Orléans, Blois, Tours, Vierzon, Saint-Nazaire, Nantes, Cholet, La Roche-sur-Yon, Poitiers, Châteauroux, Nevers, Dijon, Besançon, Mâcon, Bourg, Chambéry, Grenoble, Annecy, Zürich, Bern, Luzern, Lausanne, Genève, Neuchâtel, Basel, Freiburg, La Rochelle, Saintes, Angoulême, Limoges, Périgueux, Brive-la-Gaillarde, Clermont-Ferrand, Aurillac, MASSIF CENTRAL, Saint-Étienne, Lyon, Villeurbanne, Vichy, Montluçon, Cahors, Agen, Montauban, Albi, Pointe de la Coubre, Bordeaux, Bergerac, Mont-de-Marsan, Biarritz, Pau, Tarbes, Toulouse, Carcassonne, Narbonne, Perpignan, PYRENEES, Cap de Creus, Montpellier, Nîmes, Alès, Avignon, Montélimar, Valence, Aix-en-Provence, Marseille, Toulon, Cannes, Nice, Golfe du Lion, Mt. Blanc 15,771, Monte Viso 12,602, Monte Rosa 14,691

Turin (Torino), Novara, Bergamo, Milan (Milano), Brescia, Verona, Piacenza, Alba, Savona, Genoa (Genova), Imperia, La Spezia, Parma, Modena, Bologna, Livorno, Pisa, Florence (Firenze), Ravenna, Piombino, Siena, Grosseto, Perugia, Civitavecchia, ROME, ISOLA D'ELBA, Golfo di Genova, Monte Rotondo 8,602, Ajaccio, Bastia, Cap Corse, Str. of Bonifacio, Sassari, Capo Caccia, Alghero, Nuoro, Olbia, Capo Comino, Oristano, Iglesias, Cagliari, Capo Carbonara, Capo Spartivento, Punta La Marmora 6,017

Esbjerg, Kolding, Odense, Copenhagen (København), Flensburg, Schleswig, Kiel, Lübeck, Itzehoe, Cuxhaven, Wilhelmshaven, Bremerhaven, HAMBURG, Bremen, Oldenburg, Leeuwarden, Groningen, Den Helder, Haarlem, Amsterdam, Leiden, The Hague ('s-Gravenhage), Utrecht, Rotterdam, Nijmegen, Osnabrück, Münster, Dortmund, Wuppertal, Düsseldorf, Essen, Hannover, Bielefeld, Hildesheim, Kassel, Göttingen, Erfurt, Leipzig, Eisenach, Suhl, Coburg, Brugge, Gent, Antwerpen, Maastricht, BRUSSELS (Bruxelles), Namur, Charleroi, Liège, Mons, Köln, Bonn, Siegen, Koblenz, Wiesbaden, Mainz, Frankfurt, Offenbach, Mannheim, Würzburg, Heidelberg, Heilbronn, Karlsruhe, Pforzheim, Saarbrücken, Trier, Luxembourg, Stuttgart, Augsburg, Regensburg, Ulm, Memmingen, Kempten, Garmisch-Partenkirchen, Innsbruck, Baden-Baden, Böblingen, Dachau, Chur, Merano, Bolzano, Trento, Cuneo, Coni

Cabo Ortegal, La Coruña, El Ferrol del Caudillo, Cabo de Finisterra, Cabo de Peñas, Gijón, Oviedo, Santander, Vigo, Pontevedra, Ourense, Lugo, Ponferrada, León, Palencia, Burgos, Vitoria, Bilbao, Donostia, Pamplona, Logroño, CORDILLERA CANTÁBRICA, Braga, Porto, Aveiro, Coimbra, Salamanca, Zamora, Valladolid, Segovia, Soria, Zaragoza, Huesca, Lleida, Sabadell, BARCELONA, Mataró, Tarragona, Girona, SISTEMA IBÉRICO, SPAIN, MADRID, Alcalá de Henares, Getafe, Plasencia, Cáceres, Toledo, Aranjuez, Cuenca, Castelló de la Plana, València, Tomelloso, Puertollano, Albacete, Alacant, Elx, Murcia, Cartagena, Cabo de Palos, Cabo de la Nau, Gandia, Cabo de Gata, Almería, Motril, Málaga, Granada, SIERRAS BÉTICAS, Úbeda, Jaén, Córdoba, Écija, Sevilla, Huelva, Faro, Olhão, SIERRA MORENA, Antequera, Lorca, Badajoz, Mérida, Évora, Setúbal, Lisbon (Lisboa), Cabo da Roca, Cabo Espichel, PORTUGAL, Cabo de São Vicente, Cádiz, Jerez de la Frontera, Algeciras, GIBRALTAR (U.K.), Strait of Gibraltar, Ceuta (Sp.), Melilla (Sp.), Golfo de Cádiz

BALEARIC ISLANDS (Sp.), Palma, MALLORCA, MENORCA, EIVISSA, Eivissa, Artà, FORMENTERA, Cap de Ses Salines, Cap de Barbaria

Tanger, Tétouan, Larache, Kenitra, Rabat, CASABLANCA, Meknes, Fès, Taza, Khouribga, Oujda, Nador, Al Hoceima, Ouezzane, Sidi bel Abbès, Mestghanem, Wahran (Oran), DAHRA, Aïn Témouchent, ATLAS MOUNTAINS, ALGIERS (EL DJAZAÏR), Tizi Ouzou, Boumerdes, Bouira, El Boulaïda, Bejaïa, Sétif, Skikda, Qacentina (Constantine), Annaba, Guelma, Souk Ahras, El Kef, Tunis, Nâbeul, Sousse, Kairouan, Kalaa, Tbessa, Khenchla, Batna, Bou Saâda, El Djelfa, Aïn el Beïda, Béja, Cap Bon, Sfax, Mechriyya, Khounga

Scale 1:10,000,000; one inch to 158 miles
Lambert Conformal Conic Projection

0 50 100 150 200 250 300 Miles

0 100 200 300 400 500 Kilometers

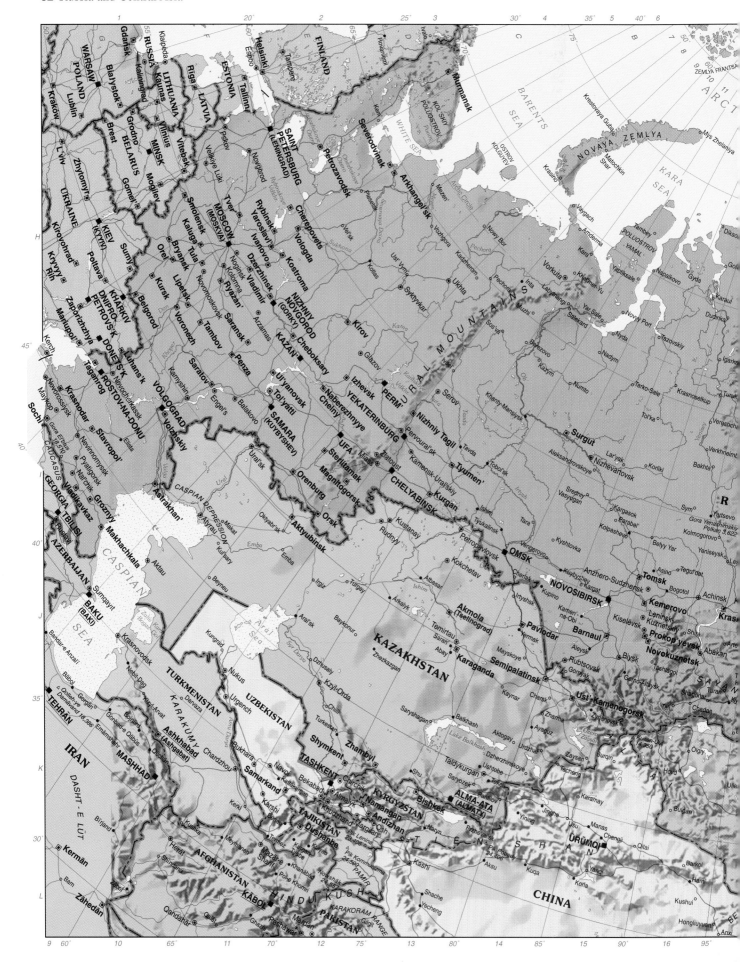

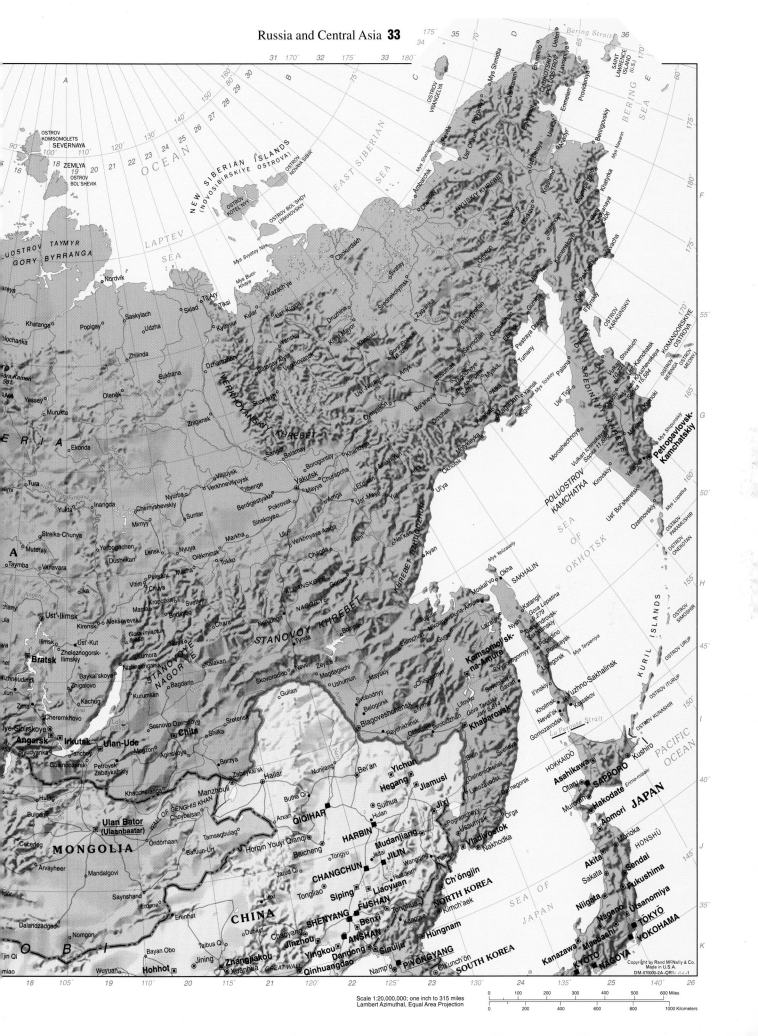

Tropic of Cancer

OKINO-TORI-SHIMA
(Japan)

MAUG ISLANDS

A

20°

**PHILIPPINE
SEA**

**NORTHERN MARIANA
ISLANDS
(U.S.)**

MARIANA

ISLANDS

SARAGON

B

15°

SAIPAN

GUAM
(U.S.)   Agana

PACIFIC   OCEAN

C

10°

Legaspi

PHILIPPINES

SAMAR

Tacloban

LEYTE

olod

Cebu

Tagbilaran

aguete

Buluan

Sibuyan Sea

Cagayan de Oro

Maravi   Bislig

MINDANAO

ato   Mount
Apo
9,692   **Davao**

Koronadal   Cape San Agustin

General Santos

Tinaca
Point

YAP

SOROL

GAFEKUT

**FEDERATED STATES OF
MICRONESIA**

D

PALAU ISLANDS

Koror

SONSORAL
ISLANDS

PALAU (BELAU)

5°

KEPULAUAN
TALAUD

Tahuna

C A R O L I N E   I S L A N D S

E

MOROTAI

Galela   Wayabula

Manado   Gunung Klabat 6,634

Tondano

talo

HALMAHERA

Weda

Molucca Sea
(Laut Maluku)

Labuha

Tanjung Libobo

M
O
L
U
C
C
A
S

Laiwui

KEPULAUAN OBI

KEPULAUAN SULU

Ceram Sea

PULAU MISOOL
(Laut Seram)

Sorong
Jazirah Doberai

Kokas

Manokwari

Bosnik

Teba

Tanjung D'Urville

Serui   Sarmi

Waren

MANUS
ISLAND   Patusi

Kavieng

Equator

0°

Namlea
BURU

Piru   CERAM (SERAM)   Bula

Ambon

S

I

A

Teluk
Cenderawasih

Semenanjung
Bomberai

PEGUNUNGAN   MAOKE

Puncak
Jaya
16,503

Puncak
Trikora
15,584

Puncak
Mandala
15,677

Mamberamo

Jayapura

Wewak

NEW   GUINEA

Sepik

CENTRAL RANGE

Bogia

Madang

B I S M A R C K   A R C H I P E L A G O

Hoskins

Aisega

Awul

NEW BRITAIN

5°

Tual

Dobo

Banda Sea
(Laut Banda)

(MALUKU)

KEPULAUAN BARAT DAYA

Tepa

Birab

KEPULAUAN
ARU

Kepi

Tanjung De Jongs

Digul

Lake
Murray

Mount
Hagen

Mount
Wilhelm
14,793

Goroka

Mount
Giluwe
14,330

Kerema

Cape Cretin

Lae

**PAPUA NEW
GUINEA**

Losuia

Popondetta

Tufi

PULAU YAMDENA

Saumlaki

PULAU YOS
SUDARSO

Tanjung Vals

Fly

Gulf of
Papua

OWEN STANLEY RANGE

Esa'ala

Samarai

Dili

Tutuala

TIMOR

cussi

Sge

Timor Sea

ARAFURA   SEA

Merauke

Mari

Daru

Port Moresby

10°

Torres Strait

Bamaga   Cape York

H

Scale 1:16,000,000; one inch to 252 miles
Sinusoidal Projection

0   100   200   300   400   500 Miles

0   200   400   600   800 Kilometers

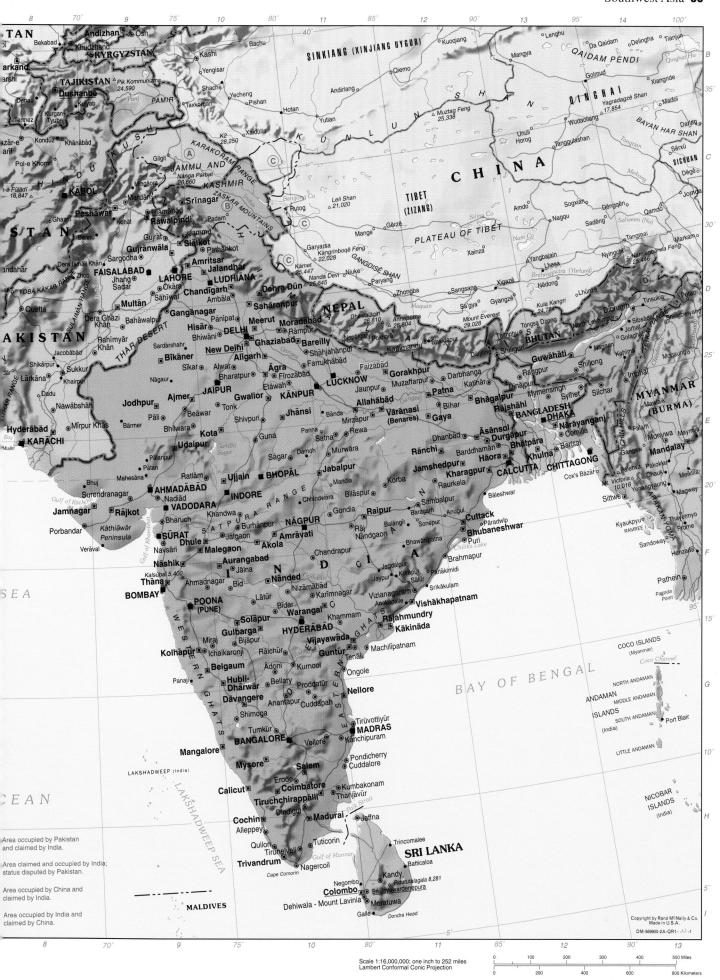

Area occupied by Pakistan
and claimed by India.

Area claimed and occupied by India;
status disputed by Pakistan.

Area occupied by China and
claimed by India.

Area occupied by India and
claimed by China.

Scale 1:16,000,000; one inch to 252 miles
Lambert Conformal Conic Projection

DM-569900-2A-QR1- -1

0   100   200   300   400   500 Miles

0   200   400   600   800 Kilometers

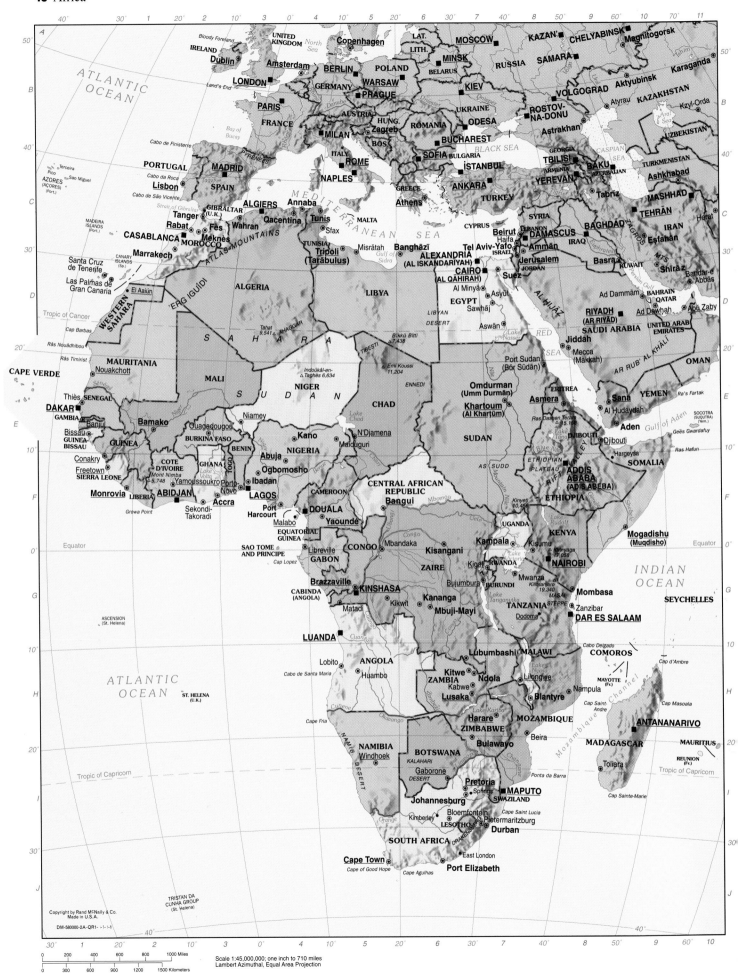

Scale 1:45,000,000; one inch to 710 miles
Lambert Azimuthal, Equal Area Projection

Scale 1:20,000,000; one inch to 315 miles
Sinusoidal Projection

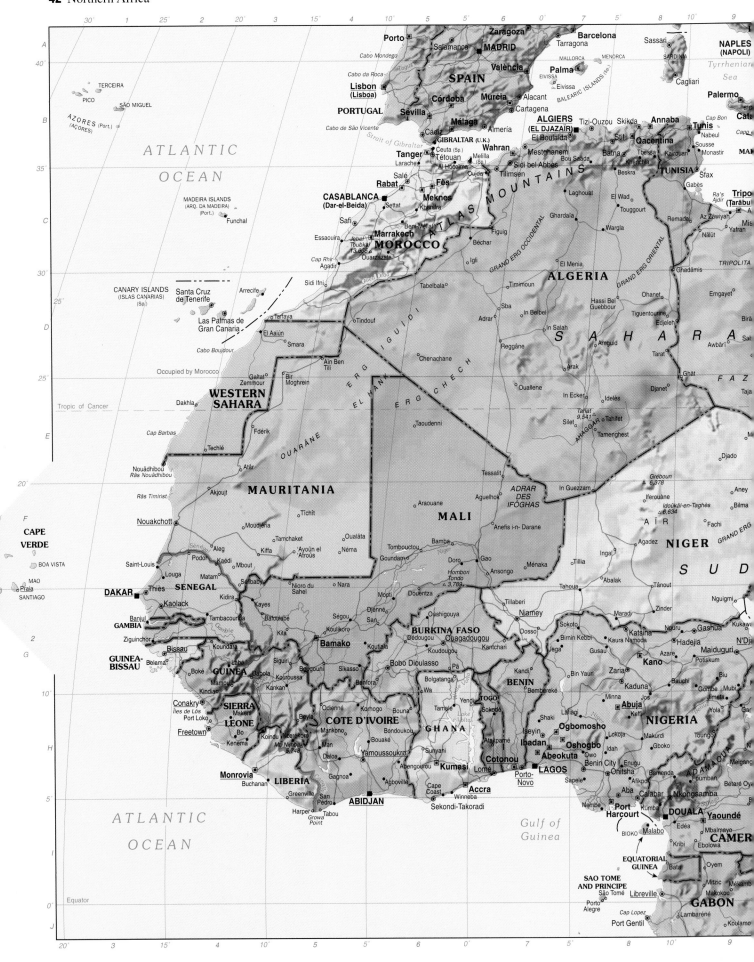

ATLANTIC OCEAN

Tyrrhenian Sea

AZORES (Port.)
(AÇORES)

TERCEIRA
PICO
SÃO MIGUEL

MADEIRA ISLANDS
(ARQ. DA MADEIRA)
(Port.)
Funchal

CANARY ISLANDS
(ISLAS CANARIAS)
(Sp.)
Santa Cruz de Tenerife
Las Palmas de Gran Canaria
Arrecife

Tropic of Cancer

CAPE VERDE
BOA VISTA
MAO
Praia
SANTIAGO

Porto
Lisbon (Lisboa)
PORTUGAL
Cabo Mondego
Cabo da Roca
Cabo de São Vicente
Salamanca
MADRID
SPAIN
Córdoba
Sevilla
Cádiz
Strait of Gibraltar
GIBRALTAR (U.K.)

Zaragoza
València
Murcia
Málaga
Almería
Alacant
Cartagena

Barcelona
Tarragona
MALLORCA
Palma
EIVISSA
Eivissa
BALEARIC ISLANDS (Sp.)
MENORCA

Sassari
SARDINIA
Cagliari

NAPLES (NAPOLI)
Palermo

ALGIERS (EL DJAZAÏR)
El Boulaïda
Tizi-Ouzou
Skikda
Annaba
Tunis
Cap Bon
Nabeul

Tanger
Ceuta (Sp.)
Tétouan
Al Hoceïma
Melilla (Sp.)
Larache
Rabat
Salé
Fès
Meknes
CASABLANCA (Dar-el-Beida)
Settat
Khenifra
Safi
Essaouira
Marrakech
Jebel Toubkal 13,665
MOROCCO
Cap Rhir
Agadir
Ouarzazate
Oued Draa
Sidi Ifni
Tarfaya

Wahran
Mestghanem
Sidi bel Abbes
Tilimsen
Oujda
Figuig
Béchar
Igli
Tabelbala
ATLAS MOUNTAINS

Bou Saâda
Batna
Stif
Qacentina
TUNISIA
Sfax
Gabès
Ra's Ajdir

Laghouat
El Wad
Touggourt
Ghardaïa
El Menia
GRAND ERG OCCIDENTAL
GRAND ERG ORIENTAL
Wargla
Ghadâmes
TRIPOLITA
Tripoli (Ṭarābulu)

Beskra
Khenchla
Tbessa
Kairouan
Sousse
Monastir
MAH

ALGERIA
Timimoun
Sba
In Belbel
Reggâne
Adrar
In Salah
Hassi Bel Guebbour
Ohanet
Tiguentourine
Edjeleh
SAHARA

Emgayet
Birâ
Sab
Awbârî

Smara
El Aaiún
Cabo Boujdor
WESTERN SAHARA
Occupied by Morocco
Dakhla

Cap Barbas

Nouâdhibou
Râs Nouâdhibou
Ras Timirist

Nouakchott

Galtat Zemmour
Bir Moghrein
Fdérik
Techlé
Atâr
Akjoujt

MAURITANIA
Moudjéria
Tâmchaket
Tîchît
'Ayoûn el 'Atroûs
Néma
Oualâta

Tindouf
ERG IGUIDI
EL HANK
ERG CHECH
Chenachane
Ouallene
Taoudenni
Araouane

Tessalit
In Guezzam
ADRAR DES IFÔGHAS
Aguelhok

In Ecker
Arak
Silet
Tahat 9,541
AHAGGAR
Tamenghest
Idelès
Tahifet

Djanet
Ghât
FAZ
Taja

Grebou 6,378
Djado
Aney
Iferouâne
Idoûkâl-en-Taghès 6,634
Bilma

Anefis i-n- Darane

MALI
Araouane
Timbuktu
Goundam
Bamba
Gao
Ménaka
Ansongo

Tahoua
Abalak
Tânout
Fachi
AÏR
Agadez
NIGER
GRAND ERG

SUD

Nioro du Sahel
Nara
Hombori Tondo 3,789
Doro
Aleg
Kiffa
Kaédi
Mbout
Podor
Saint-Louis
Louga
Thiès
DAKAR
Kaolack
Banjul
GAMBIA
Ziguinchor
Bissau
GUINEA-BISSAU
Bolama
Boké

SENEGAL
Matam
Sélibaby
Kidira
Kayes
Bafoulabé
Tambacounda
Kita
Koundara
Labé
Mamou
Kindia
Conakry
Îles de Lôs
Port Loko
Freetown

Nioro du Sahel
Séfou
Nara
Ségou
Douentza
Mopti
San
Djénné
Kayes
Kita
Koulikoro
BAMAKO
Koutiala
Siguiri
Kouroussa
Kankan
Bougouni
Dabola
GUINEA
Beyla
Mt Nimba 3,748
Kindu Nzérékoré
Man
Odienné
Korhogo
Sikasso
Bobo Dioulasso
Banfora
Mankono
Bouaké
Bouna

Tillaberi
Niamey
Ouahigouya
Dédougou
BURKINA FASO
Ouagadougou
Koudougou
Kantchari
Dosso
Fada N'Gourma
Pâ
Bolgatanga
Wa
Yendi
Tamale
TOGO
Sokodé
Atakpamé
GHANA
Sunyani
Kumasi

Maradi
Sokoto
Birnin Kebbi
Kaura Namoda
Gusau
Kandi
Kaduna
Zaria
Bin Yauri
Jega
BENIN
Bembéréké
Parakou
Minna
Lafiagi
Shaki
Iseyin
Oyo
Ogbomosho
Ibadan
Oshogbo
Lokoja
Idah
Abeokuta
LAGOS
Porto-Novo
Cotonou
Lomé

Zinder
Ngourti
Nguru
Hadejia
Azare
Kano
Katsina
Gashua
Kukawa
N'Djamena
Maiduguri
Potiskum
Biu
Gombe
Mubi
Bauchi
Jimeta
Yola
Toungo
ABUJA
Jos
Keffi
Makurdi
Enugu
Onitsha
Afikpo
Aba
Calabar
NIGERIA
Benin City
Owo
Sapele
Warri
Nembe
Port Harcourt

COTE D'IVOIRE
Yamoussoukro
Daloa
Gagnoa
Abengourou
Agboville
ABIDJAN
San Pédro
Harper
Tabou
Growa Point
Bondoukou
Sunyani
Cape Coast
Sekondi-Takoradi
Accra
Winneba

LIBERIA
Monrovia
Buchanan
Greenville

SIERRA LEONE
Makeni
Bo
Kenema
Koidu

ATLANTIC OCEAN

Gulf of Guinea

BIOKO
Malabo
EQUATORIAL GUINEA
Bata
SAO TOME AND PRINCIPE
São Tomé
Oyem
Mitzic
Mékambo
Makokou

Port Harcourt
Kumba
Mbalmayo
DOUALA
Edéa
Yaoundé
CAMER
Kribi
Ebolowa
Mbalmayo
Bamenda
Foumban
Kribi
ADAMAOUA
Bétaré-Oya
Meiganga
Nkongsamba
Kumba

GABON
Libreville
Porto Alegre
Cap Lopez
Port Gentil
Lambaréné
Koulamo

Equator

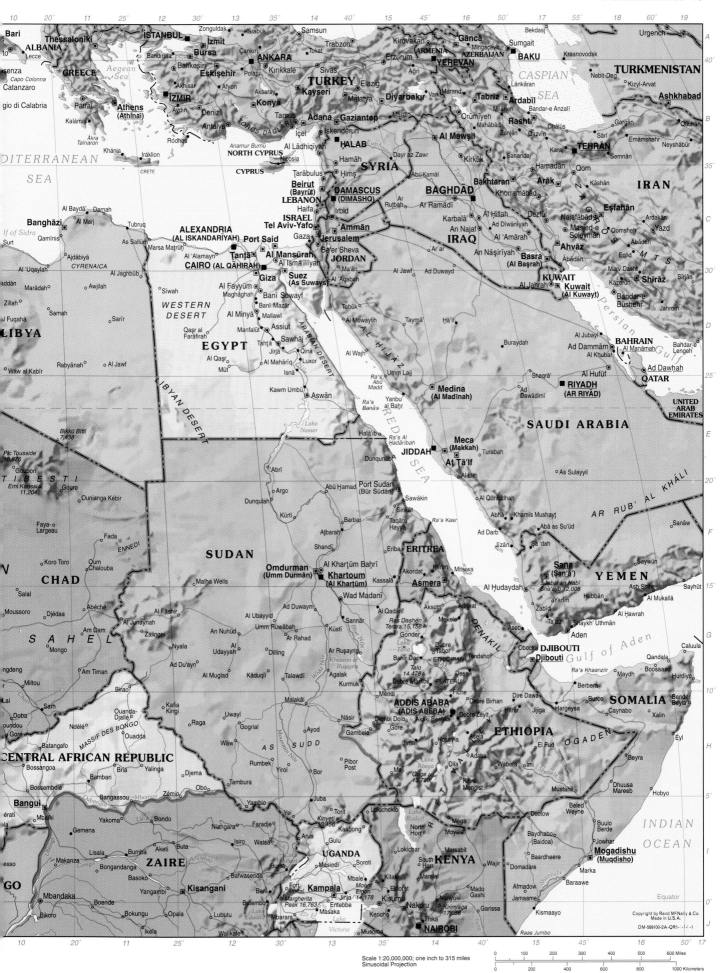

Bari
ALBANIA
Thessaloniki
Lecce
GREECE
enza
Catanzaro
gio di Calabria
Capo Colonna
Kalámi
Pátrai
Athens
(Athínai)
Ákra
Tainaron
ITERRANEAN
SEA
CRETE
Khánia
Iráklion
Ródhos

İSTANBUL
İzmit
İzmir
Bursa
Bandırma
Balıkesir
Akhisar
Aydın
Denizli
Antalya
Anamur Burnu
İçel
TOROS DAĞLARI

Zonguldak
Karabük
Çankırı
ANKARA
Polatlı
Eskişehir
Kırıkkale
Afyon
Aksaray
Konya
Tarsus
Adana
Al Lādhiqīyah

Samsun
Trabzon
Tokat
Sivas
Kayseri
TURKEY
Malatya
Gaziantep
İskenderun
HALAB
Hamāh
Himş
NORTH CYPRUS
Nicosia
CYPRUS
Tel Aviv-Yafo
Ţarābulus
Beirut
(Bayrūt)
LEBANON
Haifa

Kırovakan
Erzurum
Ağrı
Diyarbakır
Van
Mardin
Dayr az Zawr
SYRIA
Abū Kamāl
DAMASCUS
(DIMASHQ)
Ar
Rutbah
Ar Ramādī

Gäncä
ARMENIA
YEREVAN
AZERBAIJAN
Marand
Tabrīz
Mīāneh
Bandar-e Anzalī
Al Mawşil
Kirkūk
Sanandaj
BAGHDAD
Khorramābād
Karbalā'
An Najaf

Sumgait
BAKU
Krasnovodsk
Lānkāran
Ardabīl
Rasht
Qazvīn
Karaj
Hamadān
Arāk
Bākhtarān
Qom
Kāshān

Urgench
CASPIAN
SEA
Nebit-Dag
Gorgān
Emāmshahr
Semnān
TEHRĀN
IRAN
Eşfahān

TURKMENISTAN
Kızyl-Arvat
Ashkhabad
Qūchān
Neyshābūr
Mashhad

ALEXANDRIA
(AL ISKANDARĪYAH)
Port Said
Ţanţā
Al Manşūrah
CAIRO (AL QĀHIRAH)
Al Ismā'īlīyah
Giza
Suez (As Suways)
Al Fayyūm
Banī Suwayf
WESTERN
DESERT
Maghāghah
Banī Mazār
Al Minyā
Mallawī
Manfalūţ
Assiut
Qaşr al
Farāfirah
Sawhāj
Ţahţā
Jirjā
Qina
Luxor
EGYPT
Al Qaşr
Al Mahārīq
Mūţ
Isnā
Kawm Umbū
Aswān
Lake
Nasser

Jerusalem
Be'er Sheva
Gaza
ISRAEL
JORDAN
Amman
Irbid
Ma'ān
Al 'Aqabah
Tabūk
Al Muwayliḩ
Al Wajh

Ad Duwayd
Al Jawf

Al Jawf
Al Ḩillah
Ad Dīwānīyah
An Nāşirīyah
Basra
(Al Başrah)
IRAQ
An Najaf
Al 'Amārah
Ar'ar

Dezfūl
Masjed-e
Soleymān
Ahvāz
Ābādān
Eqlīd
Kāzerūn
Shīrāz

Najafābād
Qomsheh
Ābādeh
Yazd
Ardakān
Mārv Dasht
Sīrjān

KUWAIT
Al Jahrah
Kuwait
(Al Kuwayt)
Persian
Gulf
Al Jubayl
Ad Dammām
Al Khubar
Al Hufūf
BAHRAIN
Al Manāmah
Ad Dawḩah
QATAR
UNITED
ARAB
EMIRATES
Bandar-e
Būshehr
Jahrom
Bandar-e
Lengeh
Ra's
Madd
Taymā'
Ḩā'il
Buraydah
Ad
Dawādīmī
Shaqrā'
RIYADH
(AR RIYĀD)
SAUDI ARABIA

Medina
(Al Madīnah)
Yanbu'
al Baḩr
Ra's
Banās
Ra's Abu
Madd
RED
SEA
Halā'ib
Ra's Al
Hadāribah
Dunqunāb
JIDDAH
Meca
(Makkah)
At Ţā'if
Al Līth
Turabah
As Sulayyil
Al Qunfudhah
Abā as Su'ūd
Abhā
Khamis Mushayţ
Ad Darb
Jīzān
Şa'dah
AR RUB' AL KHĀLI
Sanāw

Sana
(Şan'ā')
Jabal an Nabī
Shu'ayb 12,008
Ḩabbān
Yarīm
Zabīd
Ta'iz
Shaykh 'Uthmān
Aden
Ash Shiḩr
Al Mukallā
Sayḩūt
Saywūn
YEMEN

If of Sidra
Surt
Banghāzī
Al Marj
Al Baydā'
Darnah
Tubruq
CYRENAICA
Al 'Uqaylah
Ajdābiyā
Qamīnis
addān
Marādah
Awjilah
Zillah
Samāḩ
Sarīr
Al Jaghbūb
Sīwah
Marsa Maţrūḩ
As Sallūm
Al 'Alamayn
Al Jawf
Al Fuqahā
Rabyānah
Al Jawf
Waw al Kabīr
LIBYA
LIBYAN DESERT
ARABIAN DESERT

Bikkū Bitti
7,438
Pic Toussside
10,876
Goubon
TIBESTI
Emi Koussia
11,204
Gouro
Ounianga Kébir
Faya-
Largeau
Fada
ENNEDI
Koro Toro
Oum
Chalouba
CHAD
Salal
Moussoro
Abéché
Djédaa
Am Dam
Zalingei
Al Junaynah
SAHEL
Mongo
Al Fāshir
Mélha Wells
Ad Duwaym
SUDAN
Omdurman
(Umm Durmān)
Al Kharţūm Baḩrī
Khartoum
(Al Kharţūm)
Kassalā
Wad Madanī
Al Qadārif
ERITREA
Akordat
Keren
Mitsiwa
Asmera
Sana

DJIBOUTI
Djibouti
Obock
Aseb
DENAKIL
Tendaho
Gulf of Aden
Qandala
Boōsaaso
Ra's Khaanzīir
Maydh
Berbera
Burco
SOMALIA
Bender
Beyla
Calula

Nyala
An Nuhūd
Umm Ruwābah
Ar Rahad
Al
Udayyah
Ad Du'ayn
Dilling
Kādugli
Talawdī
Ar Ruşayriş
(Khazzan ar
Ruşayriş)
Agalak
Kurmuk
Méndi
ADDIS ABABA
(ADIS ABEBA)
Mekele
Adīgrat
Aksum
Adwa
Gonder
Lake
Tana
Bahir Dar
Dābre
Tabor
ETHIOPIAN
Talo
14,478 ▲
Dese
Débre Markos
PLATEAU
Fiche
Débre Birhan
Debre Zeyit
Akāki Beseka
Harar
Jijiga
Hargeysa
ETHIOPIA
OGADEN
Dhuusa
Mareeb
Hobyo
Beyra
Eyl

Bifao
Miltou
Sarh
AS SUDD
Mongo
Am Timan
Kafia
Kingi
Raga
Nyala
Kurmuk
Malakāl
Nāşir
Gambéla
Jima
Hosaina
Āwasa
Goba
El Fud
Adaba
Wabera
Ilmi
Shebeli
Mustahīl
Beled
Weyne
Buulo
Berde

CENTRAL AFRICAN REPUBLIC
Bossangoa
MASSIF DES BONGO
Ndélé
Ouanda-
Djallé
Ouadda
Batangafo
Bria
Yalinga
Bambari
Bossembélé
Bangassou
Zémio
Obo
Djema
Tambura
Yambio
Rumbek
Yirol
Bor
Pibor
Post
Mountain Nile
Ayod
Waw
Gogrial
Uwayl
Mou
13,780 ▲
Guge
Lake
Chamo
Dila
Kibre
Mengist
Mega
Doolow
Baydhabo
(Baidoa)
Baardheere
Jowhar
Mogadishu
(Muqdisho)
INDIAN
OCEAN

Bangui
érati
la
Mbaïki
Gemena
Mbandaka
Boende
Bikoro
Bokungu
Lisala
Bumba
Bongandanga
Basoko
Aketi
Buta
Kisangani
Yangambi
Opala
Ikela
Walikale
ZAIRE
Makanza
Basankusu
Bafwasende
Watsa
Isiro
Niangara
Faradje
Bondo
Aru
Gulu
Arua
Yei
Torit
Juba
Kinyeti
10,456 ▲
Lokichokio
Kaabong
North
Horr
South
Horr
Maralal
UGANDA
Entebbe
Fort
Portal
Margherita
Peak 16,763
Mbarara
Masaka
Jinja
Kampala
Masindi
Soroti
Kitale
Eldoret
Lake
Edward
Lake
Victoria
Musoma
Mbale
Mount
Elgon
14,178 ▲
Bunia
Kericho
Kisumu
Nakuru
KENYA
Nanyuki
Kirinyaga
17,058 ▲
Wajir
Marsabit
Mado
Gashi
Garissa
Jamaame
Afmadow
Kismaayo
Raas Jumbo
Marka
Baraawe
NAIROBI
Thika
Equator

Moyale
Mega
Dambi Dolo
Góre
Mendi
Maji

Copyright by Rand McNally & Co.
Made in U.S.A.
DM-589100-2A-QR1-

RUSSIA
SAKHALIN
SEA OF OKHOTSK
Poluostrov Kamchatka
BERING SEA
ALEUTIAN IS
International Date Line

HIMALAYAS
Kathmandu
NEPAL (BHU.)
INDIA
BNGL.
CHITTAGONG
MYANMAR (BURMA)
YANGON
THAILAND
BANGKOK
CAMBODIA
Phnum Pénh
THANH PHO HO CHI MINH (SAIGON)
Mui Ca Mau

CHINA
XI'AN
Chongqing
WUHAN
NANJING
SHANGHAI
Yangtze
GUANGZHOU
Da Nang
Ha Noi
MACAO (Port.)
HONG KONG (U.K.)
KAOHSIUNG
T'AIPEI
TAIWAN
Hai Phong
HAINAN DAO
Viangchan
LAOS
VIETNAM
Da Nang

BEIJING
SHENYANG
TIANJIN
NORTH KOREA
P'YŎNGYANG
SEOUL
QINGDAO
SOUTH KOREA
PUSAN
KITAKYŪSHŪ
KŌBE
Fuji-san 12,388
TOKYO
YOKOHAMA

Vladivostok
SAPPORO
HOKKAIDO
KURIL ISLANDS
SEA OF JAPAN
JAPAN
HONSHŪ
KYŪSHŪ

PACIFIC

Tropic of Cancer

SOUTH CHINA SEA

Escarpada Point
LUZON
PHILIPPINE SEA
MANILA
QUEZON CITY
PHILIPPINES
Cebu
Zamboanga
MINDANAO
Davao
Bandar Seri Begawan
BRUNEI
Gunong Kinabalu 13,455

MALAYSIA
Kuala Lumpur
SINGAPORE
BORNEO (KALIMANTAN)
Gunung Kerinci 12,467
SUMATRA
PALEMBANG
Banjarmasin
CELEBES
CERAM
JAKARTA
SURABAYA
JAVA
INDONESIA
TIMOR

CHRISTMAS ISLAND (Austl.)
TIMOR SEA
Darwin
Cape Londonderry
Cape Leveque

GUAM (U.S.)
NORTHERN MARIANA ISLANDS (U.S.)
MARIANA ISLANDS
Koror
PALAU ISLANDS
PALAU (BELAU)
FEDERATED STATES OF MICRONESIA
CAROLINE ISLANDS
MICRONESIA
MARSHALL ISLANDS
KIRIBATI
Equator

NAURU
MELANESIA
NEW GUINEA
Puncak Jaya 16,503
Mt. Giluwe 14,330
NEW BRITAIN
PAPUA NEW GUINEA
Port Moresby
Tanjung Vals
Cape York
ARAFURA SEA
BOUGAINVILLE
SOLOMON ISLANDS
Honiara
SANTA CRUZ ISLANDS
TUVALU
WALLIS AND FUTUNA (Fr.)
PHOENIX
KIR
TO
WES
SA

Cape York
Cape York Peninsula
Gulf of Carpentaria
Normanton
Cooktown
Cairns
Townsville
CORAL SEA
VANUATU
Port Vila
NEW CALEDONIA (Fr.)
NOUVELLE CALÉDONIE
Noūméa
FIJI
VANUA LEVU
VITI LEVU
Suva
TO

GREAT DIVIDING RANGE
GREAT SANDY DESERT
Alice Springs
AUSTRALIA
Ayers Rock 2,844
GREAT VICTORIA DESERT
Carnegie
Carnarvon
Tropic of Capricorn
North West Cape
INDIAN OCEAN
Kalgoorlie-Boulder
Wanneroo
Perth
Cape Arid
Great Australian Bight
Cape Naturaliste
Point D'Entrecasteaux
Hood Point
Cape Carnot
Port Augusta
Adelaide
Cape Jaffa
Darling
Mt. Kosciusko 7,310
Melbourne
Cape Otway
Cape Portland
Cape Grim
TASMANIA
Mt. Ossa 5,305
Hobart
South East Cape

Sandy Cape
Cape Capricorn
Brisbane
NORFOLK ISLAND (Austl.)
Newcastle
Sydney
Canberra
TASMAN SEA
Cape Howe

Copyright by Rand McNally & Co.
Made in U.S.A.
DM-514200-2A-QR1-

North Cape
Auckland
NORTH ISLAND
East Cape
Mt. Ruapehu 9,177
Cape Farewell
SOUTH ISLAND
Wellington
NEW ZEALAND
Christchurch
CHATHAM ISL
Mt. Cook 12,316
Cape Providence
STEWART ISLAND

UNITED STATES

12 160° 13 150° 14 140° 15 130°

VANCOUVER ISLAND

Seattle
Portland
ROCKY MOUNTAINS
Denver
St. Louis
Cape Fear
ATLANTIC OCEAN
SIERRA NEVADA
UNITED STATES
Albuquerque Memphis Atlanta
Jacksonville
San Francisco
DALLAS
Appalachian Mountains
Cape Canaveral
OCEAN
LOS ANGELES
Tucson
El Paso
San Antonio
HOUSTON
Tampa
Miami BAHAMAS
SAN DIEGO
Cape Sable
Baja California
Gulf of Mexico
MONTERREY
HAVANA
CUBA
Punta Eugenia
Golfo de California
Rio Grande
Tropic of Cancer
Cabo San Lucas
MEXICO
San Luis Potosí
Tampico
Mérida
Yucatán Peninsula
CARIBBEAN SEA
JAMAICA
Kingston
HAWAIIAN ISLANDS (U.S.)
GUADALAJARA
MEXICO CITY PUEBLA
BELIZE
Honolulu OAHU MAUI
Acapulco
GUATEMALA
Honduras
Tegucigalpa
HAWAII Hilo
GUATEMALA
EL SALVADOR NICARAGUA
San Salvador
Managua
COSTA RICA
San José

LINE ISLANDS
POLYNESIA
Equator
GALAPAGOS ISLANDS
(ARCHIPIÉLAGO DE COLÓN)
(Ecuador)
Punta Galera
QUITO
ECUADOR
GUAYAQUIL
NORTHERN COOK ISLANDS
MARQUESAS ISLANDS
(ÎLES MARQUISES)
Punta Pariñas
Chiclayo
PERU
AMERICAN SAMOA
Nev. Huascarán 22,133
COOK ISLANDS (N.Z.)
TUAMOTU ARCHIPELAGO
FRENCH POLYNESIA
Punta Lachay
Callao
Lima
Papeete TAHITI
SOUTHERN COOK ISLANDS
Punta Carreta
Punta Parada
PITCAIRN (U.K.)
Arequipa
Tropic of Capricorn
EASTER ISLAND
(ISLA DE PASCUA)
(Chile)
CHILE
PACIFIC OCEAN
ARGENTINA
Valparaíso
CÓRDOBA
Santiago

12 160° 13 150° 14 140° 15 130° 16 120° 17 110° 18 100° 19 90° 20 80° 21 70° 22 60°

Scale 1:45,000,000; one inch to 710 miles
Lambert Azimuthal, Equal Area Projection

0 200 400 600 800 1000 Miles
0 300 600 900 1200 1500 Kilometers

SOLOMON SEA

NEW BRITAIN

Cape Cretin

Lae

Popondetta

OWEN STANLEY RANGE

Port Moresby

Kulumadau

Samarai

BOUGAINVILLE

CHOISEUL

SANTA ISABEL

SOLOMON ISLANDS

Honiara

MALAITA

GUADALCANAL

SAN CRISTOBAL

CORAL SEA

SANTA CRUZ ISLANDS

TUVALU

VANUATU

ÎLES BANKS

ESPIRITU SANTO

PENTECATE

MALAKULA

EPI

Port Vila

ÉFATÉ

NEW

ERROMANGO

HEBRIDES

WALLIS AND FUTUNA (Fr.)

FIJI

VANUA LEVU

Lautoka

VITI LEVU

Suva

KANDUVU ISLAND

NEW CALEDONIA (Fr.)

NOUVELLE CALÉDONIE

LOYALTY ISLANDS

Nouméa

BARRIER REEF

Halifax Bay

Townsville

le Frere

rns

Mackay

Mt. Dalrymple 4,131

Blair Athol

Rockhampton

Emerald

Gladstone

Springsure

Theodore

Bundaberg

Mitchell

Chinchilla

Maryborough

Sandy Cape

FRASER ISLAND

Gympie

Mt. Kiangarow 3,760

Redcliffe

Toowoomba

Ipswich

Brisbane

Warwick

Southport

Cape Byron

DARLING DOWNS

Lismore

Grafton

Armidale

Coffs Harbour

Nyngan

Tamworth

Dubbo

Taree

WALES

Cessnock

Newcastle

Penrith

Parramatta

Sydney

Campbelltown

Goulburn

Wollongong

A.C.T.

Canberra

Cooma

Mt. Kosciusko 7,310

Cape Howe

Sale

PACIFIC

OCEAN

NORFOLK ISLAND (Austl.)

TASMAN

SEA

Wilsons Promontory

FLINDERS ISLAND

Cape Portland

Launceston

TASMANIA

Freycinet Peninsula

South East Cape

Cape Maria van Diemen

North Cape

Cape Brett

Whangarei

Needles Point

Mount Roskill

East Coast Bays

Manukau

Auckland

Hamilton

Bay of Plenty

Tauranga

Albatross Point

NORTH ISLAND

Rotorua

East Cape

New Plymouth

Cape Egmont

Mt. Ruapehu

Taupo

Gisborne

Wanganui

Napier

Cape Farewell

Palmerston North

Hastings

The Twins 5,990

Cape Foulwind

Porirua

Greymouth

Nelson

Wellington

SOUTH ISLAND

NEW ZEALAND

SOUTHERN ALPS

Haast

Jackson Head

Waitaki

Christchurch

West Cape

Manapouri

Ashburton

Timaru

Invercargill

Oamaru

Foveaux Strait

Dunedin

STEWART ISLAND

CHATHAM ISLANDS (N.Z.)

Tropic of Capricorn

International Date Line

Scale 1:20,000,000; one inch to 315 miles
Lambert's Azimuthal; Equal Area Projection

| 0 | 100 | 200 | 300 | 400 | 500 | 600 Miles |

| 0 | 200 | 400 | 600 | 800 | 1000 Kilometers |

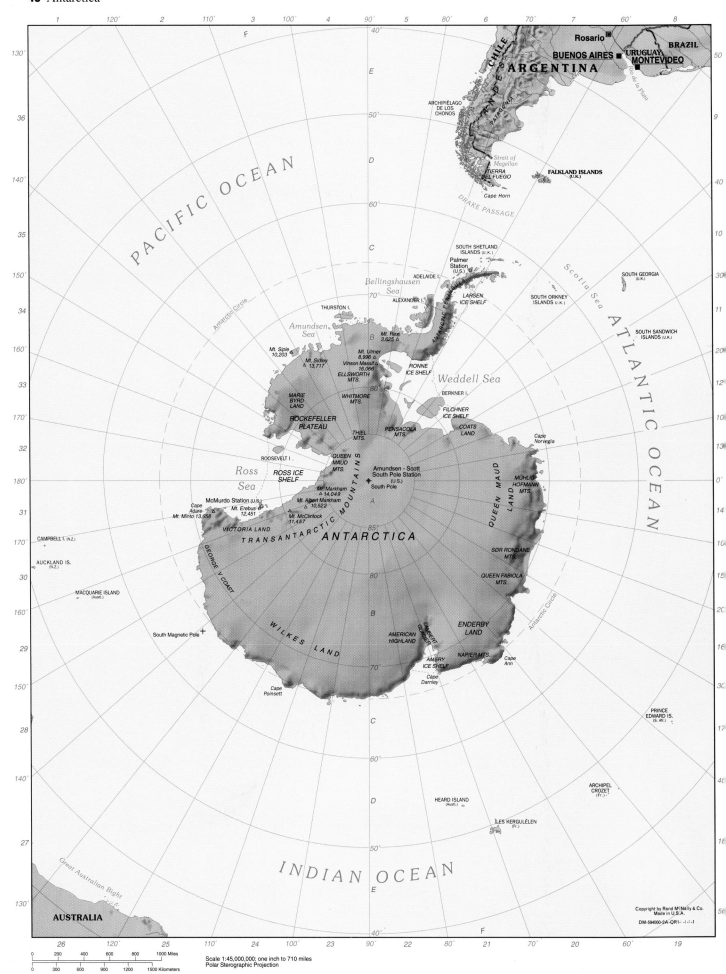

PACIFIC OCEAN

Rosario

BUENOS AIRES **URUGUAY** **BRAZIL**
ARGENTINA **MONTEVIDEO**

CHILE

ARCHIPIÉLAGO
DE LOS
CHONOS

PATAGONIA

Strait of
Magellan

TIERRA
DEL FUEGO

FALKLAND ISLANDS
(U.K.)

Cape Horn

DRAKE PASSAGE

Scotia Sea

ATLANTIC OCEAN

SOUTH SHETLAND
ISLANDS (U.K.)

Palmer
Station
(U.S.)

ADELAIDE I.

SOUTH GEORGIA
(U.K.)

Bellingshausen
Sea

LARSEN
ICE SHELF

SOUTH ORKNEY
ISLANDS U.K.

SOUTH SANDWICH
ISLANDS (U.K.)

THURSTON I.

ALEXANDER I.

Amundsen
Sea

Mt. Rex
3,625

Mt. Siple
10,203

Mt. Ulmer
8,996

RONNE
ICE SHELF

Weddell Sea

Mt. Sidley
13,717

Vinson Massif
16,066

ELLSWORTH
MTS.

BERKNER I.

Cape
Norvegia

MARIE
BYRD
LAND

WHITMORE
MTS.

FILCHNER
ICE SHELF

COATS
LAND

ROCKEFELLER
PLATEAU

PENSACOLA
MTS.

THIEL
MTS.

ROOSEVELT I.

QUEEN
MAUD
MTS.

Amundsen - Scott
South Pole Station
(U.S.)
South Pole

QUEEN MAUD LAND

MÜHLIG-
HOFMANN
MTS.

Ross
Sea

ROSS ICE
SHELF

Mt. Markham
14,049

Mt. Albert Markham
10,522

TRANSANTARCTIC MOUNTAINS

McMurdo Station (U.S.)

Cape
Adare
Mt. Minto 13,658

Mt. Erebus
12,451

Mt. McClintock
11,457

SØR RONDANE
MTS.

CAMPBELL I. (N.Z.)

VICTORIA LAND

ANTARCTICA

QUEEN FABIOLA
MTS.

AUCKLAND IS.
(N.Z.)

GEORGE V COAST

ENDERBY
LAND

MACQUARIE ISLAND
(Austl.)

WILKES LAND

AMERICAN
HIGHLAND

LAMBERT GLACIER

NAPIER MTS.

Cape
Ann

South Magnetic Pole

AMERY
ICE SHELF

Cape
Darnley

PRINCE
EDWARD IS.
(S. Afr.)

Cape
Poinsett

Antarctic Circle

ARCHIPEL
CROZET
(Fr.)

HEARD ISLAND
(Austl.)

ÎLES KERGUÉLÉN
(Fr.)

Great Australian Bight

INDIAN OCEAN

AUSTRALIA

Antarctic Circle

Copyright by Rand McNally & Co.
Made in U.S.A.
DM-594000-2A-QR1- -I-I-1

0   200   400   600   800   1000 Miles
0   300   600   900   1200   1500 Kilometers

Scale 1:45,000,000; one inch to 710 miles
Polar Sterographic Projection

Index

Abbreviations of Geographical Names and Terms

Ab., Can. . . . . Alberta
Ak., U.S. . . . . Alaska
Al., U.S. . . . . Alabama
Ant. . . . . Antarctica
Ar., U.S. . . . . Arkansas
Arg. . . . . Argentina
Asia . . . . Asia
Austl. . . . . Australia
Az., U.S. . . . . Arizona
b. . . . . bay, gulf
Bah. . . . . Bahrain
B.C., Can.
British Columbia
Bol. . . . . Bolivia
Braz. . . . . Brazil
c. . . . . cape, point
Ca., U.S. . . . . . . California
Can. . . . . Canada
Cay.Is. . . . . Cayman Islands
C.Iv. . . . . Cote d'Ivoire
Co., U.S. . . . . Colorado
Col. . . . . Colombia
cont. . . . . continent

C.R. . . . . Costa Rica
Ct., U.S. . . . . Connecticut
ctry. . . . . country
D.C., U.S.
District of Columbia
De., U.S. . . . . Delaware
dep. . . . . dependency
Dom. Rep.
Dominican Republic
El Sal. . . . . El Salvador
Eng., U.K. . . . . . . England
Eur. . . . . Europe
Falk. Is. . . . . Falkland Islands
Fl., U.S. . . . . Florida
Ga., U.S. . . . . Georgia
Guad. . . . . Guadeloupe
hist. reg. . . . . historic region
H.K. . . . . Hong Kong
Hond. . . . . Honduras

i. . . . . island
Ia., U.S. . . . . Iowa
Id., U.S. . . . . Idaho
Il., U.S. . . . . Illinois
In., U.S. . . . . Indiana
Indon. . . . . Indonesia
I. of Man . . . . . Isle of Man
Ire. . . . . Ireland
is. . . . . islands
Jam. . . . . Jamaica
Ks., U.S. . . . . Kansas
Ky., U.S. . . . . . . Kentucky
l. . . . . lake
La., U.S. . . . . . . Louisiana
Leb. . . . . Lebanon
Ma., U.S. . . Massachusetts
Malay. . . . . Malaysia
Md., U.S. . . . . Maryland
Me., U.S. . . . . Maine
Mex. . . . . Mexico
Mi., U.S. . . . . . . Michigan

Mn., U.S. . . . . . Minnesota
Mo., U.S. . . . . Missouri
Mong. . . . . Mongolia
Monts. . . . . Montserrat
Mor. . . . . Morocco
Moz. . . . . Mozambique
Ms., U.S. . . . . . Mississippi
Mt., U.S. . . . . Montana
mth. . . . . river mouth
mtn. . . . . mountain
mts. . . . . mountains
N.A. . . . . North America
Nb., U.S. . . . . . . Nebraska
N.B., Can.
New Brunswick
N.C., U.S.
North Carolina
N.D., U.S. . . North Dakota
Newf., Can.
Newfoundland
N.H., U.S.
New Hampshire
Nic. . . . . Nicaragua

N. Ire., U.K.
Northern Ireland
N.J., U.S. . . . . . New Jersey
N.M., U.S. . . . New Mexico
N.S., Can. . . . Nova Scotia
Nv., U.S. . . . . Nevada
N.W.T., Can.
Northwest Territories
N.Y., U.S. . . . . . New York
N.Z. . . . . New Zealand
Oh., U.S. . . . . Ohio
Ok., U.S. . . . . . Oklahoma
Ont., Can. . . . . Ontario
Or., U.S. . . . . Oregon
Pa., U.S. . . . . Pennsylvania
Pak. . . . . Pakistan
Pan. . . . . Panama
Para. . . . . Paraguay
pen. . . . . peninsula
Phil. . . . . Philippines
plat. . . . . plateau
pol. div. . . political division
Port. . . . . Portugal

P.R. . . . . Puerto Rico
prov. . . . . province
Que., Can. . . . . Quebec
res. . . . . reservoir
S. Africa . . . . South Africa
Sask., Can.
Saskatchewan
S.C., U.S.
South Carolina
Scot., U.K. . . . . . Scotland
S.D., U.S. . . . South Dakota
Sen. . . . . Senegal
Sri L. . . . . Sri Lanka
St. K./N.
St. Kitts and Nevis
stm. . . . . river, stream
strt. . . . . strait
terr. . . . . territory
Tn., U.S. . . . . . . Tennessee
Trin.
Trinidad and Tobago

Tx., U.S. . . . . Texas
U.K. . . . . . United Kingdom
Urug. . . . . Uruguay
U.S. . . . . United States
Ut., U.S. . . . . Utah
Va., U.S. . . . . Virginia
Ven. . . . . Venezuela
vol. . . . . volcano
Vt., U.S. . . . . Vermont
Wa., U.S. . . . . Washington
W. Bank . . . . . . West Bank
Wi., U.S. . . . . . . Wisconsin
W.V., U.S. . . West Virginia
Wy., U.S. . . . . . . Wyoming

A

Aba . . . H-8 42
Abaco, i. . . . C-9 17
Ābādān . . . C-4 38
Abaetetuba . . . D-9 23
Abagner Qi . . . C-11 35
Abakan . . . G-16 32
Abalak . . . F-8 42
Abancay . . . F-4 22
Abay . . . H-12 32
Abaya, Lake . . . H-14 43
Abbeville . . . B-4 30
Abengourou . . . H-6 42
Abeokuta . . . H-7 42
Aberdeen, Scot., U.K. . . . D-5 28
Aberdeen, S.C., U.S. . . . D-7 12
Aberdeen Lake . . . D-14 6
Abidjan . . . H-6 42
Abilene . . . J-7 13
Abisko . . . B-9 28
Aborigen, Pik, mtn. . . . E-27 33
Abu Dhabi, see Abū Ẓaby . . E-5 38
Abuja . . . H-8 42
Abū Ẓaby (Abu Dhabi) . . E-5 38
Acámbaro . . . G-9 19
Acapulco . . . I-10 19
Acarai Mountains . . . C-7 23
Acarigua . . . B-5 22
Accomac . . . H-9 10
Accra . . . H-6 42
Achill Head, c. . . . E-3 28
Achinsk . . . F-16 32
Acklins, i. . . . D-10 17
Aconcagua, Cerro, mtn. . . . C-3 21
Acre, stm. . . . F-5 22
Acre, state . . . E-4 22
Actopan . . . G-10 19
Ada . . . J-8 13
Adair, Cape . . . B-19 7
Adak . . . f-15 5
Adak Island . . . f-15 5
Adamaoua, mts. . . . H-9 42
Adana . . . H-13 27
Adare, Cape . . . B-31 48
Ad Dammām . . . D-4 38
Ad Dawḥah . . . D-5 38
Addis Ababa (Adis Abeba) . . . H-14 43
Ad Dīwānīyah . . . C-4 38
Ad Duwaym . . . G-13 43
Adelaide . . . H-6 46
Adelaide, i. . . . C-7 48
Aden (ʻAdan) . . . G-4 38
Aden, Gulf of . . . G-4 38
Adirondack Mountains . . . D-9 10
Admiralty, i. . . . D-10 5
Ādoni . . . F-10 39
Adrar . . . D-6 42
Adriatic Sea . . . D-7 31
Aegean Sea . . . E-8 31
Afghanistan, ctry. . . . C-7 38
Afikpo . . . H-8 42
Afognak Island . . . D-6 5
Africa, cont. . . . F-14 3
ʻAfula . . . m-24 25
Afyon . . . H-12 27
Agadez . . . F-8 42
Agadir . . . C-5 42
Agana . . . C-11 37
Agapa . . . C-15 32
Agattu Island . . . f-13 5
Agboville . . . H-6 42
Agen . . . D-4 30
Aginskoye . . . G-20 33
Āgra . . . D-10 39
Ağrı Dağı, mtn. . . . H-14 27
Agrigento . . . E-6 31
Agrínion . . . E-8 31
Aguadulce . . . G-8 17
Agua Prieta . . . B-5 18
Aguascalientes . . . G-8 18
Aguascalientes, state . . . F-8 18
Agulhas, Cape . . . I-4 41
Ahaggar, mts. . . . E-8 42
Ahmadābād . . . E-9 39
Ahmadnagar . . . F-9 39
Ahvāz . . . C-4 38
Aiken . . . J-6 11
Aim . . . F-24 33
Aïr, mts. . . . F-8 42
Aisega . . . G-12 37
Aix-en-Provence . . . D-5 30
Ajaccio . . . D-5 30
Ajdbiyā . . . C-11 43
Ajdir, Ra's, c. . . . C-9 42
Ajmer . . . D-9 39
Ajo . . . L-8 15
Nakhon Sawan . . . B-3 36
Akimiski Island . . . F-17 7
Akita . . . D-16 35
ʻAkko . . . m-24 25
Aklavik . . . C-6 6
Akmola (Tselinograd) . . . G-12 32
Akola . . . E-10 39
Akordat . . . F-14 43
Akpatok Island . . . D-20 7
Akron . . . F-6 10
Aksu . . . C-4 34
Aktau . . . I-8 33
Aktyubinsk . . . G-12 32
Akureyri . . . B-2 28
Al Khubar . . . D-5 38
Al Mukallā . . . G-4 38
Alabama, stm. . . . K-3 11
Alabama, state . . . J-3 11
Alacant . . . E-3 30
Alacrán, Arrecife, reef . . . F-15 19
Alagoas, state . . . E-11 23
Alagoinhas . . . F-11 23
Alajuela . . . F-8 17
Al ʻAlamayn . . . C-12 43
Al ʻAmārah . . . C-4 38
Alamogordo . . . L-12 15
Alamosa . . . H-4 13
Åland (Ahvenanmaa), i. . . . C-9 29
Al ʻAqabah . . . p-24 25
Al ʻArīsh . . . n-22 25
Alaska, state . . . B-6 5
Alaska, Gulf of . . . D-7 5
Alaska Peninsula . . . D-5 5
Alaska Range, mts. . . . C-6 5
Al ʻAyn . . . E-6 38
Alba . . . D-5 30
Albacete . . . E-3 30
Albania, ctry. . . . D-7 31
Albany, Austl. . . . G-2 46
Albany, Ga., U.S. . . . K-4 11
Albany, N.Y., U.S. . . . E-10 10
Albany, Or., U.S. . . . F-3 14
Albany, stm. . . . F-17 7
Albatross Point . . . H-13 47
Al Bayḍāʼ . . . C-11 43
Albemarle Sound . . . H-8 11
Albert, Lake . . . B-6 41
Alberta, prov. . . . E-10 6
Albert Lea . . . E-10 12
Albert Markham, Mount . . . A-29 48
Albi . . . D-4 30
Ålborg . . . D-8 28
Albuquerque . . . K-11 15
Albury . . . H-8 47
Alcalá de Henares . . . D-3 30
Alchev'sk . . . C-11 31
Aldan, stm. . . . F-24 33
Aldanskoye Nagor'ye, plat. . . . F-23 33
Aleksandrovskoye . . . E-13 32
Aleksandrovsk-Sakhalinskiy . . . G-26 33
Ålesund . . . C-7 28
Aleutian Islands . . . f-14 5
Aleutian Range, mts. . . . D-5 5
Alexander Bay . . . H-3 41
Alexander Island . . . C-6 48
Alexandria (Al Iskandarīyah), Egypt . . . C-12 43
Alexandria, La., U.S. . . . K-10 13
Alexandria, Va., U.S. . . . G-8 10
Alexandroúpolis . . . D-9 31
Aleysk . . . G-14 32
Al Fāshir . . . G-12 43
Al Fayyūm . . . D-13 43
Al Fuqahā . . . D-10 43
Algeciras . . . E-2 30
Algeria, ctry. . . . D-7 42
Alghero . . . D-5 30
Algiers (El Djazaïr) . . . B-7 42
Algona . . . E-9 12
Al-Ḥijāz, region . . . D-2 38
Al Ḥillah . . . C-3 38
Al Hoceïma . . . B-6 42
Al Ḥudaydah . . . G-3 38
Al Hufūf . . . D-4 38
Alice . . . M-7 13
Alice Springs . . . E-5 46
Alīgarh . . . D-10 39
Alijos, Isla, i. . . . E-2 18
Al Ismāʻīlīyah . . . C-13 43
Al Ismāʻīlīyah . . . o-21 25
Al Jahrah . . . D-4 38
Al Jawf . . . D-11 43
Al Junaynah . . . G-11 43
Al Khalīl . . . n-24 25
Al Kharṭūm Baḥrī . . . F-13 43
Al Khums . . . C-9 42
Al Lādhiqīyah . . . B-2 38
Allahābād . . . D-11 39
Allakaket . . . B-6 5
Allegheny, stm. . . . F-7 10
Allentown . . . F-9 10
Alleppey . . . H-10 39
Alliance . . . E-5 12
Alma-Ata (Almaty) . . . I-13 32
Almalyk . . . I-11 32
Al Manāmah . . . D-5 38
Al Manṣūrah . . . C-13 43
Al Marj . . . C-11 43
Al-Mawṣil . . . B-3 38
Almenara . . . G-10 23
Almería . . . E-3 30
Al Minyā . . . D-13 43
Alor Setar . . . D-3 36
Aloysius, Mount . . . F-4 46
Alpena . . . D-5 10
Alpine . . . K-5 13
Alps, mts. . . . C-5 30
Al Qaḍārif . . . G-14 43
Al-Qāmishlī . . . B-3 38
Al Qaṣr . . . D-12 43
Alta . . . B-10 29
Alta Floresta . . . F-7 23
Alta Gracía, Arg. . . . C-4 21
Altagracia, Ven. . . . A-4 22
Altai, mts. . . . H-15 32
Altamira . . . D-8 23
Altamont . . . G-4 14
Altamura . . . D-7 31
Altay . . . B-5 34
Altiplano, plain . . . G-5 22
Alton . . . G-11 12
Altun Shan, mts. . . . D-6 34
Alturas . . . H-4 14
Altus . . . I-7 13
Al Ubayyiḍ . . . G-13 43
Al Udayyah . . . G-12 43
Alva . . . H-7 13
Alwar . . . D-10 39
Alytus . . . E-10 29
Amadeus, Lake . . . E-5 46
Amadjuak Lake . . . D-19 7
Amambai . . . A-5 21
Amam-o-shima, i. . . . F-13 35
Amapá, state . . . C-8 23
Amarillo . . . I-6 13
Amazon (Amazonas), stm. . . D-8 23
Amazonas, state . . . D-6 22
Ambāla . . . C-10 39
Ambarchik . . . D-30 33
Ambato . . . D-3 22
Ambon . . . F-8 37
Ambre, Cap d' . . . j-10 41
Ambriz . . . D-2 41
Amchitka Island . . . f-14 5
Amchitka Pass, strt. . . . f-14 5
Amderma . . . D-10 32
American Falls Reservoir . . G-8 14
American Highland . . . B-22 48
American Samoa, dep. . . . H-12 45
Americus . . . J-4 11
Amery Ice Shelf . . . C-21 48
Amiens . . . C-4 30
Amistad Reservoir . . . L-6 13
Amlia Island . . . f-16 5
ʻAmmān . . . C-2 38
Āmol . . . B-5 38
Amos . . . G-18 7
Amrāvati . . . E-10 39
Amritsar . . . C-10 39
Amsterdam . . . E-7 28
Amu Darya, stm. . . . I-10 32
Amundsen Gulf . . . B-9 6
Amundsen-Scott South Pole Station . . . A-1 48
Amundsen Sea . . . B-2 48
Amur, stm. . . . G-25 33
Anaconda . . . E-8 14
Anadyr' . . . E-33 33
Anaktuvuk Pass . . . B-6 5
Anambas, Kepulauan, is. . . E-4 36
Anantapur . . . G-10 39
Anápolis . . . G-9 23
Anchorage . . . C-7 5
Ancona . . . D-6 31
Ancud . . . E-2 21
Anda . . . B-13 35
Andaman Islands . . . C-1 36
Andaman Sea . . . C-2 36
Anderson . . . I-5 11
Andes, mts. . . . F-4 20
Andizhan . . . I-12 33
Andong . . . D-13 35
Andorra, ctry. . . . D-4 30
Andrews . . . I-5 13
Androka . . . I-9 41
Andros, i. . . . D-9 17
Aney . . . F-9 42
Angara, stm. . . . F-18 33
Ángel de la Guarda, Isla, i. . . . C-3 18
Angeles . . . B-7 36
Angers . . . C-3 30
Angmagssalik . . . C-26 7
Angola, ctry. . . . E-3 41
Angoulême . . . C-4 30
Anguilla, ctry. . . . E-12 17
Anhui, prov. . . . E-11 35
Animas Peak . . . M-10 15
Ankang . . . E-9 34
Ankara . . . H-12 27
Ann, Cape . . . C-19 48
Annaba . . . B-8 42
An Najaf . . . C-3 38
Annapolis . . . G-8 10
Annapūrna, mtn. . . . D-11 39
Ann Arbor . . . E-5 10
An Nāṣirīyah . . . C-4 38
Anniston . . . J-4 11
An Nuhūd . . . G-12 43
Anqing . . . E-11 35
Anshan . . . C-12 35